Knitting

Amazing Patterns that Everyone Can Knit

Contents

Thank you for purchasing this book. I have collected some of my favorite knitting patterns for your enjoyment. All of these patterns can be found online for free, and where possible I have given credit to the original designer. None of these patterns is my own, and I do not claim any as my own.

Knitting is a wonderful craft to learn, and in this book we'll explore some easy and intermediate patterns. We'll also spend a bit of time refreshing your skills, or if you're a beginner learning basic stitches and techniques.

Once you're finished with this book I hope you'll be ready to move onto to more challenging and advanced patterns. I feel part of the fun of knitting is creating something with your hands that is unique and one of a kind. So feel free to put your own spin on the patterns which follow. If you don't like the colors listed, use your own. If you want to change the gauge of a pattern simply move up or down a needle size.

Thanks again, and let's get started!

Chapter One – Getting Started

In this chapter we'll go over some basic information you need to know to create the patterns I've included in this book. First of course you'll need knitting needles. Needles come in straight, circular, double pointed, and cable needles. Each one has their best use, and each one come is a variety of sizes. Straight needles are good for projects like scarves and other smaller pieces. Circular and double point needles let you work larger projects such as Afghans and knitting in the round. Cable needles are used to hold stitches so you can create cables in your knitting.

Knitting Needle Sizes

Millimeter Range	U.S. Size Range
2.25 mm	1
2.75 mm	2
3.25 mm	3
3.5 mm	4
3.75 mm	5
4 mm	6
4.5 mm	7
5 mm	8
5.5 mm	9
6 mm	10
6.5 mm	10½
8 mm	11
9 mm	13
10 mm	15
12.75 mm	17
15 mm	19
19 mm	35
25 mm	50

*Letter or number may vary. Rely on the millimeter (mm) sizing.

You will also need stitch markers, a row counter, measuring tape, shears, tapestry needle, a container to store your yarn and works in progress, a knitting bag so you can take your projects with you on the road, and a good light source. The type of yarn you choose depends upon your tastes and what the pattern calls for. Yarn comes in three basic types: animal fibers, plant fibers, and synthetic. Examples of animal fibers include wool and alpaca. Cotton and bamboo are examples of plant fibers, and acrylic is one of the most popular types of synthetic yarn. You can also find blends of many different types of fibers on the market today.

Yarn also comes in different weights. Fingerling and lace yarns are very thin and delicate. These are used for lace items and very fine knitting projects. Bulky and roving yarns are the thickest and work up very quickly to give you a plush cushy feel to your knitting projects. Look at the pattern and see what weight and type of yarn is recommended before you begin. This will make a difference on how your project knits up and matches the gauge of the pattern. This handy guide from the Craft Yarn Council shows the different weights of yarn and their descriptions.

Yarn Weight Symbols

You will find a lot of information on a yarn label. On it you'll find the weight of the yarn, the type of fiber it is made from, the suggested needle size, and care instruction. Many manufacturers today don't use dye lots, but check to see if there is one on the label and if so purchase yarn from the same dye lot so that you get a uniform color. Reading and understanding yarn labels will save you from a lot of headaches and ensure you get the right yarn for your project.

 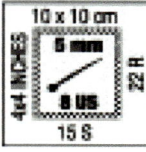 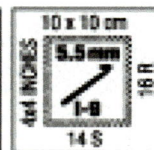  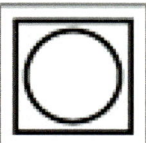

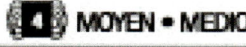

In this example you see that this yarn is a medium weight worsted yarn and size 8 knitting needles are recommended to give you a gauge of 15 stitches and 22 rows per four inch square. The yarn can be

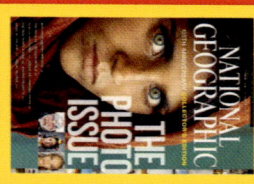

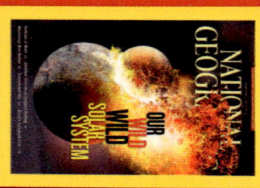

The World and All That's in It!

machine washed at no higher than 104 degrees, and tumble dried. If you purchase animal fiber yarns be very careful to check the care instructions. I would hate to spend hours working on a wool piece and then throw it in a hot dryer and have it come out ruined.

Wool and animal fibers give you a nice springy warm fabric while cotton, bamboo, and linen give you durability and pretty stitch definition. Cotton is perfect for dish and washcloths, while linen is well suited to warm weather garments since it wicks away moisture and breathes. Acrylic is a good all-purpose yarn and comes in many colors, textures, and weights. If you want to splurge try cashmere or alpaca. These yarns are soft, have a soft sheen, and give you a fabric that is very luxurious. Beware though, many knitters have found yarn addictive and their stash builds up very quickly. And yes I am guilty of this myself. This stash isn't mine, but isn't it glorious?

Chapter Two – Basic Stitches and Techniques

In this chapter we'll review basic stitches and techniques. You are probably already familiar with how to cast on, knit, purl, cable, and cast off but if you're not then this chapter will be a good starter reference for you.

Casting On

There are several methods to cast on, but I personally like the long tail method. I find it is easy and very versatile. One thing to remember is not to cast your stitches on too tightly. This will make your first row hard to knit and can cause the edge of your work to draw up. If you have a habit of casting on tightly use a size or two larger needles to cast on and then transfer the stitches to the correct size needles.

First make a slip knot and place it on your needle and leave a long tail, about 12 to 18 inches on the knot. Now hold the yarn with a loop over your thumb and over your forefinger of your left hand. Next holding the needle in your right hand bring the tip of the needle up from the bottom of the loop into the loop on your thumb and grab the yarn onto your needle. Place the tip of the needle down into the loop on your forefinger and let the loop from your thumb slip off as you pull the yarn onto the needle. Pull gently to tighten the stitch. Repeat for the correct number of stitches needed.

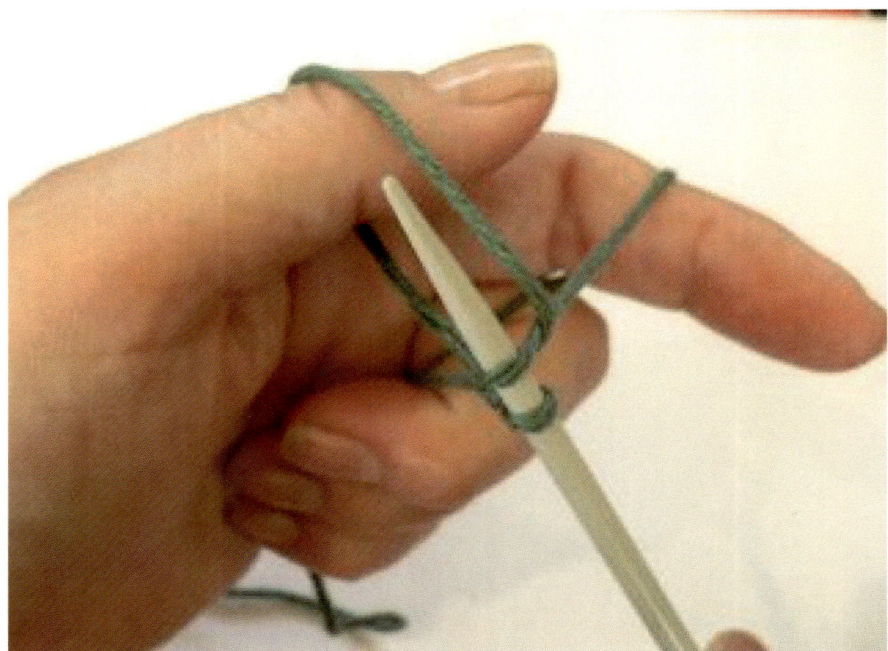

Casting Off or Binding Off

Once you finish your project you'll need to get the knitting off of the neecles. This is known as casting or binding off. When you have completed your last row start a new row and knit two stitches. Insert the left needle into the second stitch and slip it over the first stitch. Continue across the row slipping the second knit stitch over the first until you reach the last stitch. Cut the yarn and leave enough of a tail to weave in and pull the tail through the last loop on the needle.

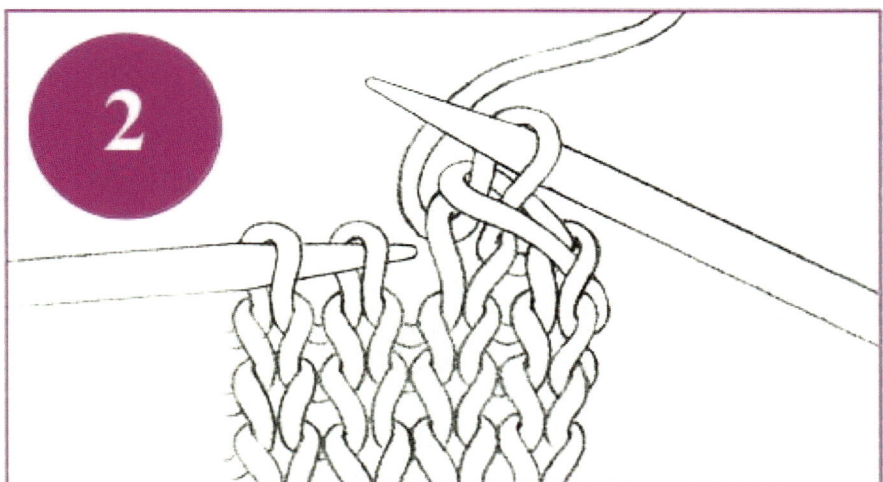

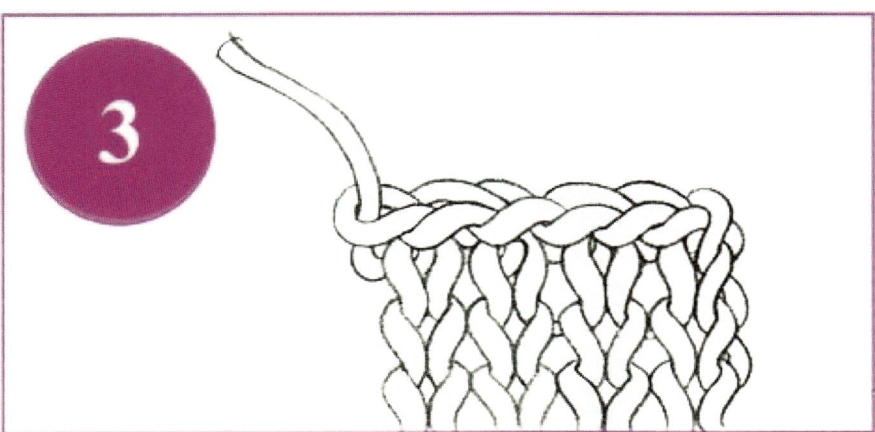

Knit and Purl Stitches

All knitting is a combination of knit and purl stitches. No matter how complex of a pattern you work with if you break it down to its most basic components you will find knit and purl stitches. It is how you combine these two stitches and how you cast your yarn over your needles or the direction you slip stitches which forms the basis for stitch patterns and combinations.

A knit stitch is done with the right needle inserted from the front into the back into the loop on your left hand needle. Bring the yarn over the needle from the back to the front and then draw this loop through the loop on the left hand needle slipping it onto the right hand needle. A knit stitch is also called a garter stitch.

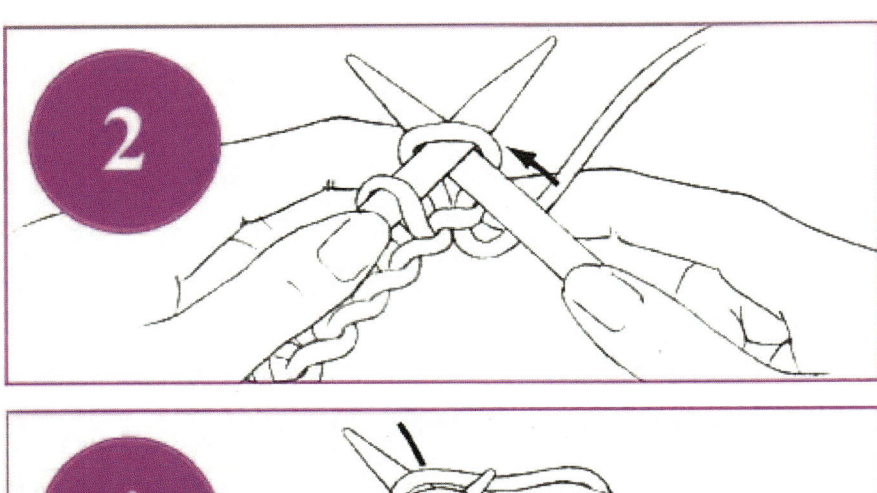

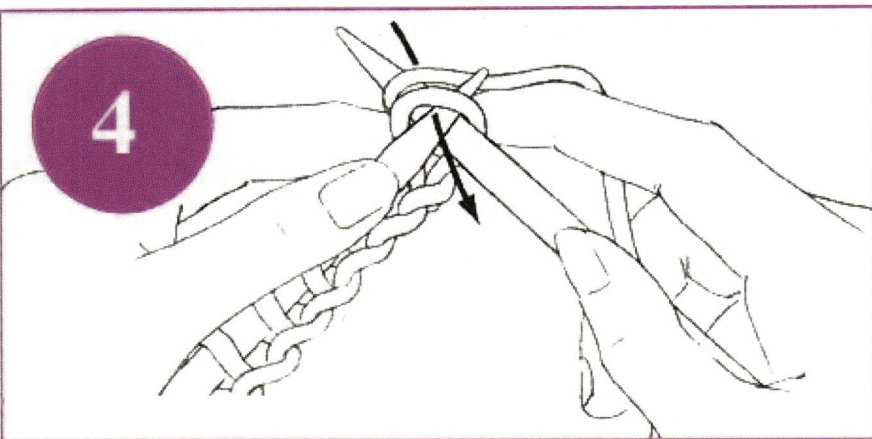

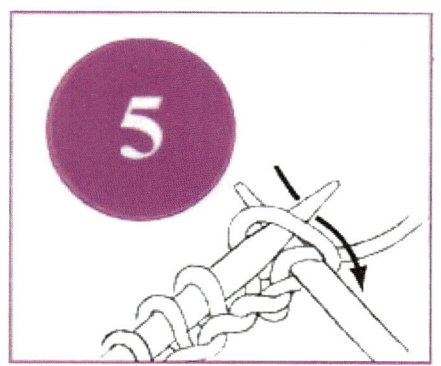

When you want to create a purl stitch the right needle is slipped into the stitch on the left needle from behind. The yarn is brought over and around the right needle and the loop is drawn through the left stitch.

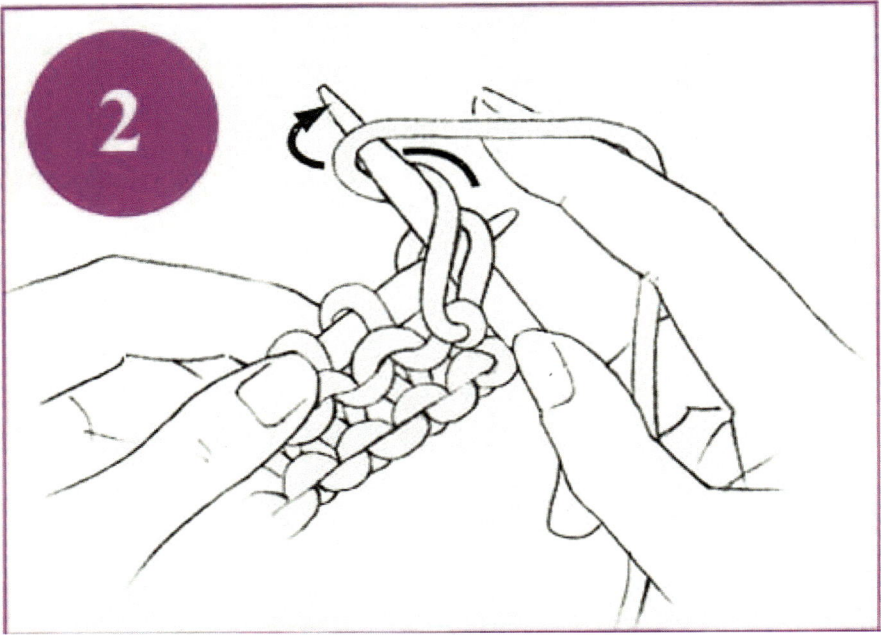

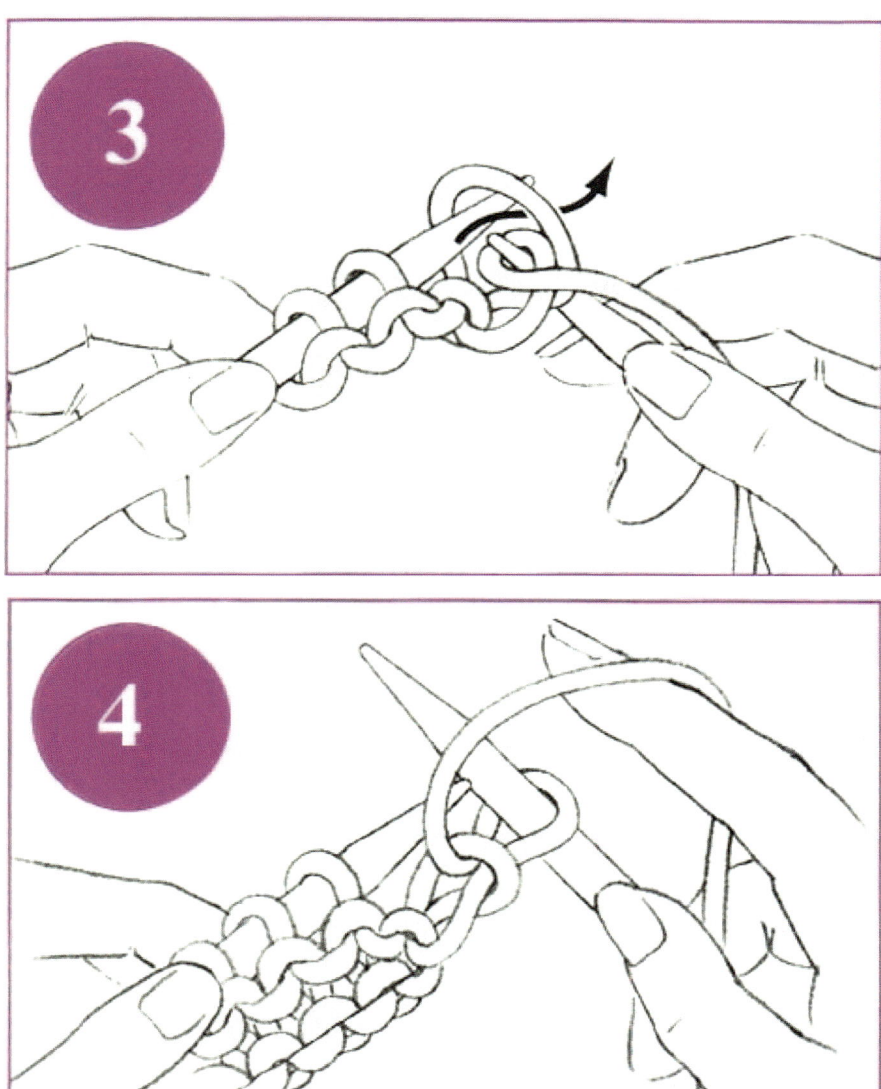

Many times a pattern will call for you to slip a stitch. This means you insert your right needle into the stitch on the left needle and simply slip it over to the right needle without doing a yarn over. The term ssk means you slip the stitch like you were going to knit by slipping the needle under the stitch from the front. Ssp means you slip the stitch as if you were going to purl the stitch by slipping the needle under the stitch from the back.

Pattern Abbreviations

This chart will give you a good reference as you work patterns. Abbreviations are used because it would make patterns much too long and complicated if every direction was written out completely.

Approx	approximately	rep	Repeat
beg	begin or beginning	Rev St st	reverse stockinette stitch
BO	bind off	RS	right side
CC	contrasting color	rnd	round
CO	cast on, cast off	sm	slip marker
cm	centimeter	SSK	slip 1, slip 1, knit two together
cn	cable needle	sl	slip
cont	continue	sl 1, k1, psso or	slip 1, knit 1, pass slipped st
dec	decrease	SKP	over
dpn	double pointed needles	st(s)	stitch(es)
eor	every other row	St st	stockinette stitch
est	established	tbl	through back loop(s)
inc	increase	tog	together
k or K	knit	WS	wrong side
k1, s1, psso	knit one, slip one, pass slipped stitch over	wyib	with yarn in back
		wyif	with yarn in front
k2tog	knit 2 together	yfon	yarn forward over needle
k2tog tbl	knit 2 together through back loop	yfrn	yarn forward and round needle
		yo	yarn over
MC	main color	yon	yarn over needle
M1	make one	yrn	yarn round needle
mm	millimeter	*	repeat instructions following or between asterisk as indicated
p or P	purl		
p2tog	purl 2 together	[ ]	repeat instructions inside brackets as indicated
p2tog tbl	purl 2 together through back loop		
pat	pattern		
pm	place marker		
psso	pass slip stitch over		
rem	remaining		

This chapter was by no means a tutorial on knitting, but more of a review and overview of the skills you will need to work the patterns in this book. (Be sure to check out my box set, The Complete Guide on How to Knit. From Beginner to Expert. Knitting for Everyone. Including Tons of Detailed Pictures: Knitting from A to Z. Take Your Skills from Basic to Advance, on Amazon if you need more detailed lessons on knitting.)

Chapter Three – Tips for Working Patterns

Learning to read and work patterns is fun. It opens up an entire world of patterns and projects for you to try. In this chapter I'll give you some handy tips to use when working patterns.

Read through the pattern before you begin. Look over the pattern completely and see if there are any stitches you don't understand or need to practice.

Check the weight and type of yarn the designer recommends. The pattern will not work up correctly if you use a much thinner or thicker yarn. The gauge will be off making the project either smaller or larger than you intended. The type of yarn is also important. Some yarns like cotton are great for summer garments and kitchen items, but acrylic or wool would not be suitable in most cases. The designer may suggest a specific brand of yarn, but as long as you substitute the same weight and fiber you can use the yarn of your choice.

Check the legend for any special symbols or abbreviations used in the pattern. More advanced patterns use charts and symbols. It is important you understand what the symbols mean. Also check to see if there are any special abbreviations the designer used. Although most patterns use the same symbols and abbreviations, patterns from other countries or older patterns may use different ones.

Always do a test swatch to measure for gauge. Gauge is very important in knitting. The pattern will tell you how many stitches and a row you should have on a 4 inch square swatch. If your swatch is larger or smaller you can either adjust your tension go up or down a needle size to obtain the correct gauge.

FINISHED MEASUREMENTS
10.5" square

YARN
Knit Picks Comfy Sport (75% Pima Cotton, 25% Acrylic; 136 yards/50g): 1 ball each of (MC) Sea Foam 24431 and (CC) White 24764.

NEEDLES
US 2 (3.0mm) 24" circular needle.

NOTIONS
Yarn needle
Stitch Marker

GAUGE
20 sts x 19 rows = 4" on US 2 needles in garter stitch.

In this example from Knit Picks Tutorials you will find all of the information you need to know about knitting this pattern. The pattern is for a dishcloth and it will be 10.5 inches square when finished. Your gauge swatch should have 20 rows with 19 stitches each when worked with a 24 inch US size 2 circular needle and Knit Picks Comfy Sport yarn.

Chapter Four – Cowls and Scarf Patterns

Scarves and hats are what most folks start with when they begin knitting. I've collected some really cute and easy patterns for you to try. All of these patterns are available for free on the internet, and if possible I have given credit to the original designers. You can find the links to all of the patterns in the Attributions section of this book. Enjoy!

Chunky Colorful Cowl

This really cute cowl is from Red Heart. It uses 2 strands of chunky yarn and large needles. It works up quickly and really gives you a chance to experiment with color combinations.

What You'll Need:

Red Heart Super Saver®: 2 skeins 3939 Blacklight (14 ounces)
Susan Bates® knitting needles: 9mm [US 13]
Yarn needle

GAUGE: 11 stitches equal 4 inches (10 cm); 17 rows equal 4 inches (10 cm) in Slip Stitch pattern.

Cowl measures 11 inches (28 cm) wide and 32 inches (81 cm) long before seaming.

PATTERN STITCHES
Slip Stitch Pattern (multiple of 2 stitches + 1)
Row 1 (WS): K1, purl to last st, K1.
Row 2: K1, *slip 1 st wyib, K1;repeat from * to end of row.
Repeat Rows 1 and 2 for pattern.

COWL
Holding two strands of yarn together, loosely cast on 31 stitches. Work Slip Stitch Pattern until
fabric measures32 inches (81 cm), ending with Row 1.Bind off all stitches loosely.

FINISHING
With yarn needle, sew cast on edge to bind off. Weave in all loose ends.

Candi's Checked Cowl

You can wear this as a cowl, or pull it up as a hooded cowl. You use two strands of yarn to work up a nice
and warm winter accessory.

What You'll Need:

3 balls of 5 ounce worsted weight yarn. Pattern uses RED HEART Soft 9925 Really Red
32 inch US size 13 (80cm) circular needle

Stitch marker and yarn needle

GAUGE: 10½ sts equal 4 inches (10 cm); 17 rounds equal 4 inches (10 cm) in Check pattern with 2 strands of yarn held together.

Cowl measures 38 inches (96.5 cm) circumference and 15 inches (38 cm) tall

Notes
1.Cowl is in the round with 2 strands of yarn throughout.
.

COWL
Loosely cast on 100 stitches with 2 strands of yarn. Place marker for beginning of round. Being careful not to twist stiches, remembering to work in the round.
Work in Garter stitch (knit every round) for 3 rounds.
Begin Check Pattern
Round 1: *K5, p5; repeat from * to end of round.
Round 2: Knit.
Rounds 3 and 4: Repeat Rounds 1 and 2.
Round 5: Repeat Round 1.
Round 6: *P5, k5; repeat from * to end of round.
Round 7: Knit.
Rounds 8 and 9: Repeat Rounds 6 and 7.
Round 10: Repeat Round 6.
Rounds 11–60: Repeat Rounds 1-10 five more times.
Working Garter stitch for3 rounds.
Bind off loosely. *FINISHING* Weave in ends.

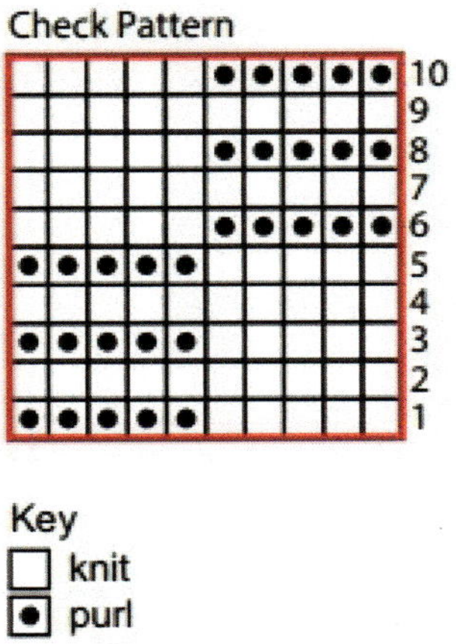

Check Pattern

Key
☐ knit
▣ purl

Survival Cowl

If you're a fan of the popular show Games of Thrones you'll want to work up this very unique cowl. You can wear this in cool weather to keep warm, or in the summer as a chic alternative to a jacket.

What You'll Need:

4 skeins of 7 ounce worsted weight yarn, pattern uses Red Heart Super Saver® in4313 Aran Fleck
32 inch size US 13 (9mm) circular needle
Ring stitch marker and detachable stitch markers, stitch holder and yarn needle

GAUGE: 10 sts equal 4 inches (10 cm); 14 rows equal 4 inches (10 cm) in Small Cable pattern. 12 stitches equal 4 inches (10 cm); 14 rows equal 4 inches (10 cm) in 1x1 Rib.

Cowl measures 36 inches (91.5 cm), unstretched, around lower edge (above Side Panel)

Notes
1. Cowl is worked in two piece, the side panel and the cowl.
2.Side Panel is worked back and forth in rows beginning at lower point of panel.
3. Cowl is worked in rounds.
4. Soild two strands of yarn throughout the entire project.

Special Stitches

kfb (Knit into front and back) equal Knit next st but do not remove from needle, knit into back loop of same st and remove from needle.

M1 equal Make 1 (Increase) – Lift strand between needles to left-hand needle and knit strand through the back loop, twisting it to prevent a hole.

RT (Right Twist) equal Knit into the front of the second stitch on the left needle leaving the stitch on the needle, knit the first stitch on the left needle, slipping both stitches off the needle.

Pattern Stitches

Small Cable Pattern (multiple of 4 stitches + 2)
Row 1 (right side): K2, *p2, RT;repeat from * to last 4 stitches, p2, k2.
Row 2: Purl.
Repeat last 2 rows for Small Cable pattern.
1x1 Rib worked in rounds (over even number of stitches)
Round 1 (right side): *K1, p1; repeat from * around.
Repeat Round 1 for 1x1 Rib.

SIDE PANEL

Cast on 4 stitches with 2 strands of yarn held together. Work in rows on circular needles, turning your work as if on straight needles.
Row 1 (right side):Kfb in each stitch across— 8 stitches.
Row 2: Purl.
Row 3:Kfb in each stitch to last st, k1—15 stitches.
Row 4: Purl.
Row 5: [K1, M1, p1]7 times, M1, k1—23 stitches.
Row 6: Purl.
Row 7: [K1, kfb, p1]7 times, k2—30 stitches.
Row 8:P15, place marker, p15.
Row 9: K2, *p2, RT;rpt from * to 1 stitch before marker, kfb, slip marker, kfb, **RT, p2; repeat from ** to last 2 stitches, k2—32 stitches.
Row 10:Purl, slipping marker as you come to it.
Row 11: K2, *p2, RT;rpt from * to 2 stitches before marker, p1, kfb, slip marker, kfb, p1, **RT, p2;repeat from ** to last 2 stitches, k2— 34 stitches.
Row 12: Purl, slipping marker as you come to it.
Row 13: K2, *p2, RT;rpt from * to 3 stitches before marker, p2, kfb, slip marker, kfb, p2, **RT, p2;repeat from ** to last 2 stitches, k2— 36 stitches.
Row 14: Purl, slipping marker as you come to it.
Row 15: K2, *p2, RT;rpt from * to 4 stitches before marker, p2, k1, kfb, slip marker, kfb, k1, p2, **RT, p2; repeat from ** to last 2 stitches, k2—38 stitches.
Row 16: Purl, slipping marker as you come to it.
Repeat Rows 9–16 until there are 76 stitches (38 stitches on each side of marker), end with a Row 14.

Divide Side Panel into Two Halves
Next Row (right side): Work Row 1 of Small Cable pattern to marker, remove marker and slip next 38 stitches on to a holder.

First Half
Continue in Small Cable pattern over the remaining 38 stitches for 7 inches (18 cm). Bind off.

Second Half

Return 38 stiches from stitch holder to needles, ready to work a right side row. Beginning with Row 1 of pattern, work in Small Cable pattern until second half measures same as first half. Bind off.

COWL

With 2 strands of yarn held together, cast on 108 stitches. Join to work in the round, taking care not to twist stitches.

Work in 1x1 Rib until piece measures about 3 inches (7.5 cm) from beginning. Decrease Round 1: [K7, k2tog] 12 times— 96 sts.

Work in 1x1 Rib for 3 inches (7.5 cm) for first pleat.

Next Round: Knit.

Work in 1x1 Rib for 1 inches (2.5 cm).

Decrease Round 2: [K6, k2tog]12 times— 84 stitches.

Work in 1x1 Rib for 3 inches (7.5 cm) for 2nd pleat.

Next Round: Knit.

Work in 1x1 Rib for 1 inches (2.5 cm).

Decrease Round 3: [K5, k2tog]12 times— 72 stitches.

Work in 1x1 Rib for 3 inches (7.5 cm) for 3rd pleat.

Bind off loosely

FINISHING

Fold each of the Cowl pleats to the outside (right side) and whip stitch the top and bottom of each pleat together on the inside (wrong side). Place two stitch markers at the two top edges of the Side Panel to the lower edge of the Cowl, leaving 2 inches (5 cm) of Cowl between the pieces for the top of armhole, then sew tope edges in place. Weave in all ends.

Simple Mobius Cowl

Mobius cowls are very trendy right now and this one is knitted up with Lion Brand silk yarn. You can use any yarn you like, but silk yarn has a slight sheen and very pretty stitch definition. The cowl is worked as one piece and then sewed to make a Mobius cowl. The yarn used in the pattern is a hand dyed silk. Sometimes the skeins will have slight differences in color. Lion Brand suggests hand winding the skeins into balls and then placing each ball into a zipped plastic bag to keep the yarn from tangling. Knit two rows from one skein, and then two rows from the next skein to blend the hand dyed color variations.

What You'll Need:

You can also substitute a less expensive yarn but just be sure it is the same weight as silk and you will need 3.5 ounces or 362 yards (100 grams or 150 meters) of yarn. The pattern is worked in 2 skeins of 492-200 LB Collection Silk Yarn in Aquarius.

US size 6 (4mm) knitting needles and a tapestry needle

GAUGE:

22 stitches plus 32 rows equal about 4 inches (10 cm) over Rows 1-8, after blocking.

STITCH EXPLANATION:

yo (yarn over)

An increase that also creates a small decorative hole (eyelet) in the fabric, worked as follows:

1. Bring yarn to front, between the needles.

2. Take yarn to back, over the right needle. This creates the new stitch. You are now ready to proceed with the next stitch as instructed.

Cowl
Loosely cast on 50 sts.
Row 1 (RS):Knit to last stitch, p1.
Row 2: Sl 1 knitwise,knit to last stitch, p1.
Row 3: Sl 1 knitwise, *k1, yo;repeat from * to last 2 stitches, k1, p1 – 97 stitches.
Row 4: Sl 1 knitwise, *k1, drop yo from previous row; rep from * to last 2 stitches, k1, p1 – 50 stitches.
Rows 5-8: Sl 1 knit wise, knit to last st, p1.
Rep Rows 3-8 until piece measures about 34 in. (86.5 cm).
Bind off loosely.

FINISHING
Soak piece in warm water for about 20 minutes. Lift carefully from water, then roll in a towel to remove excess water.
On a flat, pinnable surface, stretch damp piece to finished measurements and pin in place. Allow to dry, then unpin. Fold piece in half and turn one end of piece to add a half twist to form Mobius. Keeping the twist in place, sew the cast-on edge to the bound off edge.
Weave in ends.

Mobius Tube Scarf

This scarf is constructed as a single piece, twisted and then sewn together. It is worked in Lion Brand's beautiful Landscape yarn. Landscape yarn has a long color way which means the colors change gradually in your knitting. This is a very simple pattern, but yields stunning results.

GAUGE
11 stitches plus 14 rows equal 4 inches (10 cm) in stockinette stitch (knit 1 row, purl 1 row) using size 13 (9 mm) knitting needles.

What You'll Need:

2 skeins of Lion Brand Landscape yarn or 3.5 ounces (100 grams) of 50% wool and 50% Acrylic blend yarn in a medium weight.
US size 13 (9mm) knitting needles
Tapestry needle

Make a slip knot and place first stitch on needle. For a total of 18 stitches, cast on 17 stitches.
Knit 6 rows (equal 3 garter stitch ridges).
Work in stockinette stitch for 6 rows.

Repeat last 12 rows until piece measures 38 inches or all yarn except 24 inches is used.
Bind off all stitches loosely.
Fold scarf, giving one end a 180degree turn. Join short ends.
Weave in ends.

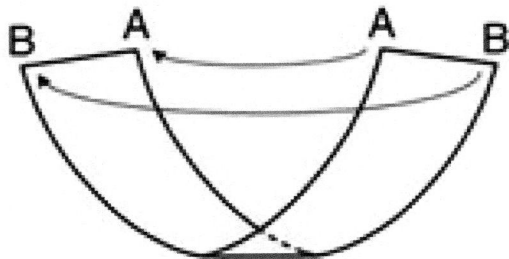

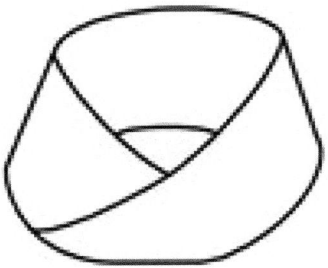

Basket weave Scarf

This scarf looks like it was hard to create, but it's really very easy. The basket weave pattern is created by sets of knit and purl stitches. You can vary this pattern by using a thinner or thicker yarn, and by using a variegated yarn for a very pretty look.

What You'll Need:

2 balls of RED HEART Grande™; pattern uses Wintergreen 511
US 19 (15mm) knitting needles
US K – 10.5 (6.5mm) crochet hook for making fringe and weaving in ends
Yarn needle

GAUGE: 6 sts equal 4 inches (10 cm); 10 rows equal 4 inches (10 cm) in Basket weave pattern. CHECK YOUR GAUGE. Use
any size needles to obtain the gauge.

Scarf measures 6 x 58 inches (15 x 147.5 cm), not including fringe.

SCARF
Cast on 9 sts.
Knit 1 row.
Row 1 (right side): K3, p3, k3.
Row 2: P3, k3, p3.

Rows 3 and 4: Repeat Rows 1 and 2.
Row 5: P3, k3, p3.
Row 6: K3, p3, k3.
Rows 7 and 8: Repeat Rows 5 and 6.
Repeat Rows 1–8until piece measures about 58 inches (147.5 cm) from beginning.
Bind off loosely.

FINISHING
Use crochet hook to weave in ends.

Fringe
Cut 16 strands of yarn, each 12 inches (30.5 cm) long. Hold 2 strands together and fold in half. Insert crochet hook in one short edge of Scarf and place fold on hook. Draw fold through edge, forming a loop. Thread ends of strands through loop and pull to tighten fringe. Repeat this process to attach 4 fringes evenly spaced across each short edge of Scarf. Trim to even. Tie the ends of the fringe strands to prevent
fraying.

Advanced Beginner Knit Scarf

This is a very unique knit scarf from Lion Brand Yarns designed by Irina Poludnenko. The scarf is worked back and forth in rows with six different pattern stitches. Slip stitch the first row purl wise and purl one stitch on the last stitch of every row. This will keep your scarf even and create a nice even edge.

What You'll Need:

7 ounces of wool blend yarn, pattern uses Lion's Pride Woolspun 80% acrylic 20% wool in Peacock
Size 10.5 (6.5mm) knitting needles and a tapestry needle

GAUGE:
13 stitches plus 20 rows equal about 4 in. (10 cm) in Step 5 pattern.

STEP 1
Cast on 24 stitches.
Row 1 (RS): Sl 1, *k2, p2;repeat from * to last 3 stitches, k2, p1.
Row 2: Sl 1, *p2, k2; rep from * to last 3 stitches, p3.
Rows 3 and 4: Repeat last 2 rows.
Row 5: Sl 1, *p2, k2; rep from * to last 3 stitches, p3.
Row 6: Sl 1, *k2, p2; rep from * to last 3 stitches, k2, p1.

Rows 7 and 8: Rep last 2 rows.
Rows 9-24: Rep Rows 1-8 twice more.
Rows 25-28: Rep Rows 1-4.

STEP 2
Row 1 (RS): Knit.
Row 2: Knit.
Row 3: Purl.
Rows 4 and 5: Knit.
Row 6: Purl.
Row 7: Knit.
Rows 8-25: Rep Rows 2-7 three more times.
Rows 26-28: Rep Rows 2-4.

STEP 3
Rows 1-28: Sl 1, *k2, p2; rep from * to last 3 stitches, k2, p1.

STEP 4
Row 1 (RS): Sl 1, k11, p12.
Row 2: Sl 1, k10, p1, k1, p11.
Row 3: Sl 1, k9, p2, k2, p10.
Row 4: Sl 1, k8, p3, k3, p9.
Row 5: Sl 1, k7, p4, k4, p8.
Row 6: Sl 1, k6, p5, k5, p7.
Row 7: Sl 1, k5, p6, k6, p6.
Row 8: Sl 1, k4, p7, k7, p5.
Row 9: Sl 1, k3, p8, k8, p4.
Row 10: Sl 1, k2, p9, k9, p3.
Row 11: Sl 1, k1, p10, k10, p2.
Row 12: Sl 1, p11, k11, p1.
Rows 13-24: Rep Rows 1-12.

STEP 5
Rows 1-28: Sl 1, k22, p1.

STEP 6
Rows 1 and 2: Sl 1, *k1, p1;repeat from * to last stitch, p1.
Rows 3 and 4: Sl 1, *p1, k1; rep from * to last stitch, p1.
Rows 5-28: Repeat last 4 rows 6 more times.

STEP 7
Rep Step 4.

STEP 8
Rep Step 3.

STEP 9
Rep Step 2.

STEP 10

Rep Step 1.
Bind off.

FINISHING
Weave in ends.

Use the following chart to keep track of the steps while knitting this scarf.

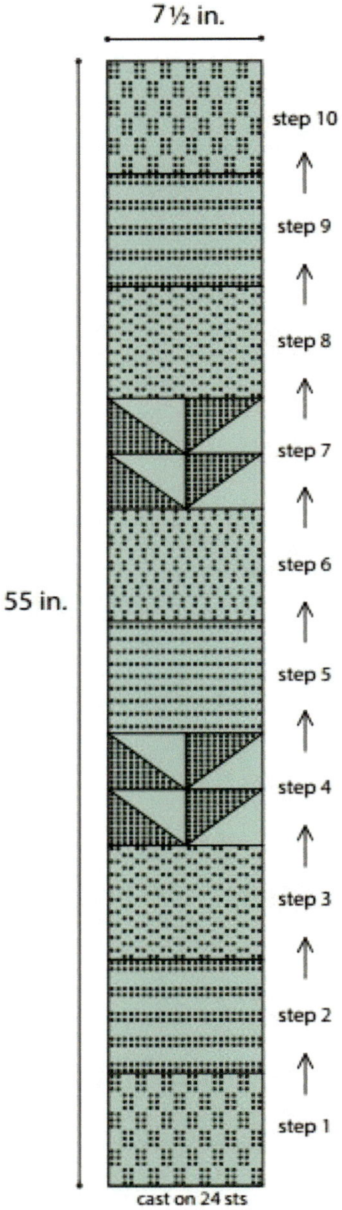

7 ½ in.

55 in.

step 10

step 9

step 8

step 7

step 6

step 5

step 4

step 3

step 2

step 1

cast on 24 sts

Reversible Cable Scarf

This scarf is made with Red Heart's stunning Boutique yarn. Similar to Lion Brand's Landscape yarn it also has a long color way and works up beautifully. There is even a Facebook page dedicated to this line of yarn from Red Heart! This scarf has a cable on both sides and is soft and long variations of color give it a very pretty striped look. This pattern can be worked from written instructions or a chart.

What You'll Need:

4 balls of RED HEART Boutique Treasure™: pattern uses Watercolors 1919
US size 9 (5.5mm) knitting needles
Cable needle, yarn needle, and a pompom make is optional

GAUGE: 18 stitches equal 4 inches (10 cm); 20rows equal 4 inches (10 cm) over 2x2 Rib. CHECK YOUR GAUGE.

Scarf measures 6 inches (15 cm) wide and 60½ inches (154 cm) long.

Special Stitches
16-st RC equal Slip 8 stitches to cable needle and hold to back of work, (K2, P2) twice, (K2, P2) twice from cable needle.
16-st LC equal Slip 8 stitches to cable needle and hold to front of work, (K2, P2) twice, (K2, P2) twice from cable needle.

Pattern Stitches

2x2 Rib (over even number of stitches)

Row 1 (right side): *K2, P2; repeat from * to end of row.

Row 2: Knit the K stitches, Purl the P stitches.

Repeat Row 2 for 2x2 Rib.

Seed Stitch

Row 1 (right side): *K1, P1; repeat from * to end of row.

Row 2: Purl the K stitches and Knit the P stitches.

Repeat Row 2 for Seed st.

SCARF

Cast on 48 stitches.

Rows 1-4: Work in Seed stitch across row.

Rows 5 and 6: Work firstitch4 stitch in Seed stitch, work40 stitches in 2x2 Rib, and work 4 stitches in Seed stitch.

Row 7: Work first 4 stitches in Seed stitch, work 20 stitches in 2x2 Rib, work 16-stitch RC, work 4 stitches in 2x2 Rib, and work 4 stitches in Seed stitch.

Rows 8-16: Work first 4 stitches in Seed stitch, work 40 stitches in 2x2 Rib, work 4 stitches Seed stitch.

Row 17: Work first 4 stitches in Seed stitch, work 8 stitches in 2x2 Rib, work 16-stitch LC, work 16 stitches in 2x2 Rib, work 4 stitches in Seed stitch.

Rows 18-24: Work first 4 stitches in Seed stitch, work 40 stitches in 2x2 Rib, work 4 stitches in Seed stitch.

Repeat Rows 5-24 until scarf measures 59½ inches (151 cm) from beginning. Work 3 rows in Seed stitch. Bind off all stitches loosely in Seed stitch.

FINISHING

With yarn needle, weave in all loose ends.

Lightly block into shape.

Optional

Make four 1 inches (2.5 cm) pompoms and attach to corners of scarf.

Pattern Chart

Key

☐ knit on right side, purl on wrong side

☐ purl on right side, knit on wrong side

16-st RC (8 over 8 2x2 rib right cross)

16-st LC (8 over 8 2x2 rib left cross)

Reversible Cable Scarf

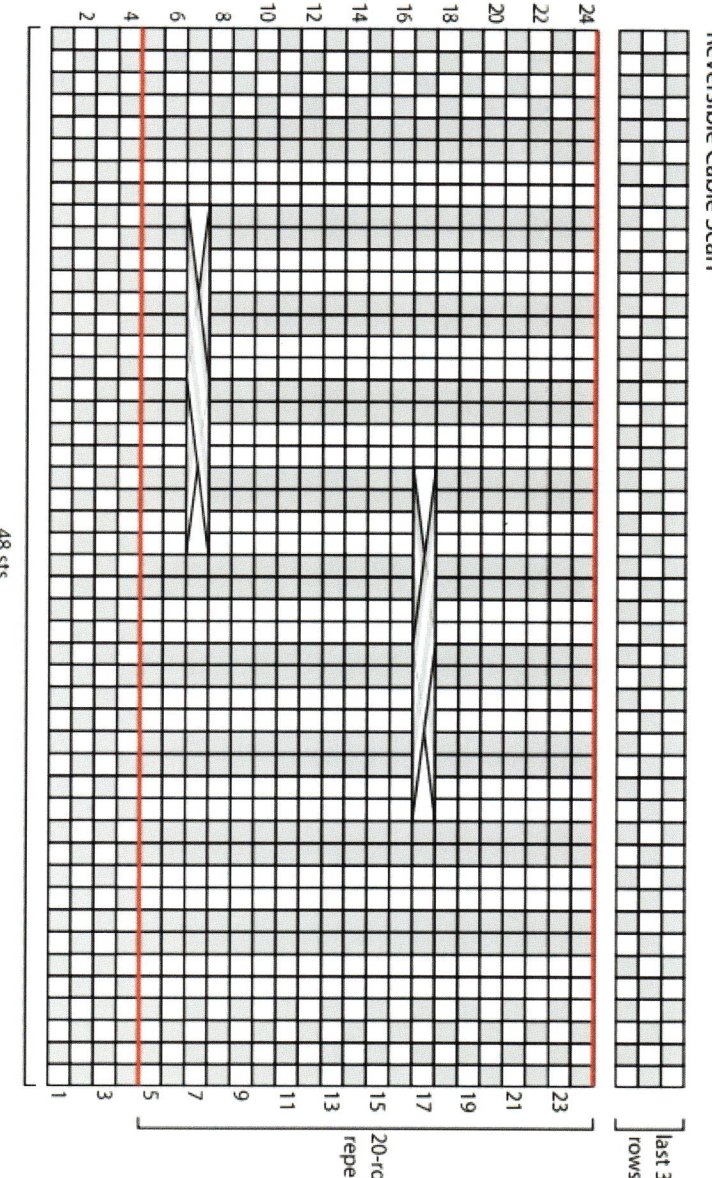

48 sts

last 3 rows

20-row repeat

Hooray Team Scarf

Red Heart Sashay yarn is a fun ruffle yarn that you can use to create scarves, accessories, and as accents on garments. If you've never worked with it, be sure to check out the video link I've included at the end of this book. You can find Sashay yarn in many different colors and types. This pattern is for a team spirit scarf that would be perfect to wear to your team's next game.

What You'll Need:

1 ball of Red Heart Boutique Sashay Team Spirit™, pattern uses 1988 Green/White
US size 9 (5.5mm) knitting needles
Sewing needle and matching thread

Gauge is not important for this pattern. Scarf measures 4 inches x 62 inches (6 inches X 38 inches)
Directions are for 62 inches scarf; changes for 38 inches long scarf are in parentheses.

NOTE
For longer scarf cast on 6 stitches; for a shorter scarf cast on 10 stitches.
Stretch one end of the Sashay open for several inches and lay it flat, placing the edge with the metallic thread along the bottom. Notice that the Sashay yarn is a mesh of holes. You will be working with the top of the mesh and leaving the metallic edge loose to form the ruffle. You are using the top railroad track of holes as if it is yarn.

SCARF

Beginning at the top right edge, insert tip of a knitting needle from back to front starting 4 inches (10 cm) from end and using top row of holes (railroad tracks). Continue inserting needle 5 (9) more times skipping 1 hole between each stitch. You now have 6 (10) cast on stitches.
Place this needle in left hand.

Pick up right hand needle and knit between the top two threads of the mesh (railroad tracks) going into every other hole.

Continue knitting these 6 (10) stitches on each row, turning your work in the same direction at end of rows.

Put your work down and open up the mesh as you go. Stop knitting when you have 24 inches (61 cm) left for binding off.

FINISHING

Bind off as usual drawing the end of the Sashay through the last bound off stitch. Trim leaving a 4 inches (10 cm) end. To finish the ends, fold under the corner and tack to inside with sewing needle and thread.

Dewdrop Scarf

This scarf is knitted with bulky yarn and a very stitch pattern. The pattern uses a lovely natural sand color, but you can use any color you like. Although the pattern specified right and wrong side, the Dewdrop stitch is so pretty you can wear it with either side as the right side.

What You'll Need

2 balls of RED HEART Medley™ bulky weight yarn, pattern uses 920 Sandy
US size 11 (8mm) knitting needles and a yarn needle

GAUGE: 12 sts equal 4 inches [10 cm]; 16 rows equal 4 inches [10 cm] in Dewdrop Stitch pattern. CHECK YOUR GAUGE. Use any size needle to obtain the gauge. Scarf measures 6½ inches wide x 59 inches long [17 cm x 150 cm].

SPECIAL STITCHES

PSSO equal Pass the slipped stitch over.
YO equal Yarn over needle.
Sl 1-K2tog-PSSO equal Slip next stitch purlwise, knit two together, pass the slipped stitch over the two knit together.
SSK equal Slip, Slip, Knit -slip next 2 stitches knitwise, then knit together.

DEWDROP STITCH PATTERN

(multiple of 6 +1)
Rows1 and 3(Wrong Side): K2 *P3, K3*, end with P3, K2
Row 2 (RS): P2 *K3, P3*, end with K3, P2
Row 4: K2 *YO, Sl 1-K2tog-PSSO, YO, K3*, end with YO, Sl 1-K2tog-PSSO, YO, K2
Rows 5 and 7: P2 *K3, P3*, end with K3, P2
Row 6: K2 *P3, K3*, end with P3, K2
Row 8: K2tog *YO, K3, YO, Sl 1-K2tog-PSSO*, end with YO, K3, YO, SSK
Repeat Rows 1-8 for Dewdrop Stitch pattern

SCARF

Cast on 21 sts.
Knit 2 rows.
Set up pattern and border on next row. First and last stitch is worked in Garter stitch for edge/border, center 19 sts are worked in Dewdrop Stitch pattern.

Row 1 (WS): K1, K2 *P3, K3*, end with P3, K2, K1.
Next Rows: Continue working in Dewdrop Stitch pattern on center 19 stiches and Garter stitch edge/border until scarf measures 58½ inches [149 cm] from cast on edge.
Next Rows: Knit 2 rows.
Next Row: Bind off all stitches knitwise.

FINISHING

With yarn needle, weave in ends. Lightly block into shape.

Chapter Five – Hat Patterns

Hats are one of the most popular knitting projects. I think it is because they are quick to work up and a great accessory. The also make quick and easy gifts. I have a big head and I find it easier to make my own hats than to try to find a ready-made one to fit my noggin. In this chapter I've searched out some really cute and fun designs for you to try. All of these patterns are found for free on the internet and I've included the links in the back of the book. I have also given credit to the original designers when I could, so have fun and enjoy!

Acorn Hat

This is a free pattern found on the Bernat website. This is a really cute hat that works up quickly. It is sized to fit an average woman's head, but you could adjust the size by using smaller or larger needles.

What You'll Need:

1 ball 10.5 ounce or 300 gram ball of bulky yarn, pattern uses Bernat® Mega Bulky™ in 88040 black.
US size 35 (19mm) needles

Gauge for pattern is 5 stitches and 7 rows equal 4inches (10 cm) in stocking stitch.

Cast on 26 stitches.
Knit 5 rows (garter stitch), noting 1st row is WS.
Next row: (RS). K7. K2tog. K8. K2tog.Knit to end of row. 24 sts.

Beg on a purl row, work even in stocking st untilHat from beg measures 8 inches [20.5 cm], ending on a purl row.

Shape top: 1st row: (RS). *K4. K2tog.Repeat from * to end of row. 20 sts.2nd and alt rows: Purl.

3rd row: *K3. K2tog. Repeat from * to end of row. 16 sts.

5th row: *K2. K2tog. Repeat from * to end of row. 12 sts.

7th row: *K1. K2tog. 8 sts.

Break yarn, leaving a long end and then draw end tightly through remaining stitches. Sew center back seam.

Holy Roller! Hat

This hat looks complicated, but is easy for the beginning knitter. The stitches combine to give the hat a very pretty texture and the brim rolls up just a bit for some extra style. I found this pattern on the Knitting with Schnapps blog through All Free Knitting and is called the No-Purl Peek-a-Boo Hat on the All Free Knitting site.

What You'll Need:

Bulky/chunky yarn with a weight of 5. The picture is done in Lion Brand's Baby Soft yarn.
10.5 Or 6.5mm circular knitting needles and double point needles

Pattern Notes:
The pattern is worked over 4 stitches, but use a multiple of 8 to keep the crown decrease the same.
To knit this using 6-weight yarn, use size 13 needles and cast on 48 stitches.
To knit this using worsted weight yarn, use size 8 needles and cast on 80 stitches.

To make it child size, use worsted yarn, size 8 needles and cast on 64 stitches. Adjust in increments of 8 stitches for individual sizes.

To knit this using sport weight yarn, use size 5 needles and cast on 112 stitches.

Pattern:

Cast on 64 stitches, place marker and join, taking care not to twist stitches.

Work Brim:
Row 1: knit all stitches
Repeat Row 1 until piece is about 3 to 4 inches.

Work Pattern:
Rows 1 & 2: knit all stitches
Row 3: *k2, k2tog, yo*; repeat around
Rows 4, 5 & 6: knit all stitches
Row 7: *k2tog, yo, k2*; repeat to end
Row 8: knit all stitches
Repeat Rows 1 - 8 until piece is about 7 to 7.5 inches in length. End on a Row 4 or 8.

Decrease Crown: use double point needles when needed
Row 1: *k6, k2tog*; repeat around
Row 2: *k5, k2tog*; repeat around
Row 3: *k4, k2tog*; repeat around
Row 4: *k3, k2tog*; repeat around
Row 5: *k2, k2tog*; repeat around
Row 6: *k1, k2tog*; repeat around
Row 7: *k2tog*; repeat around

Finish: Cut working yarn, leaving a 6-inch tail. Draw the tail through the remaining stitches, cinch closed and secure. Weave in ends.

His Skull Cap

If you're looking for a cap to knit for a man in your life, this is it. Simple ribbing stitches give the hat texture and the classic style can be worn with the brim folded up or worn straight.

What You'll Need:

1 skein of Red Heart With Love in Pewter 1401 or 1 skein of soft worsted weight yarn
US size 8 or 5mm knitting needles
Yarn needle

GAUGE: 14 stitches equal 4 inches [10 cm]; 32 rows equal 4 inches [10 cm] in Shaker Rib pattern. CHECK YOUR GAUGE.
Use any size needle to obtain the gauge.

Finished measurement: 21 inches [53 cm] circumference. Hat fits most men.

SPECIAL STITCHES

K1-B equal Knit into next st in row below.
PSSO equal Pass slipped st over.
K2tog equal Knit 2 stitches together(decrease).

PATTERN STITCHES
2x2 Rib
Row 1 (Right Side): K2, P2.
Row 2:Knit the knit stitches, and purl the purl stitches.
Repeat rows 1-2.

Shaker Rib Stitch
Row 1 (Wrong Side): Knit.
Row 2: K1, *K1-B, P1. Repeat from * to last 2
sts, K1-B, K1.
Repeat rows 1-2.

HAT
Cast on 82 stitches.
Row 1 (Right Side): Work in 2x2 Rib stitch pattern until hat measures 3 inches [8 cm] from cast-on edge.
Next Row (Right Side) Dec: Decrease 9 stitches on last row as follows: *K2tog, K8. Repeat from * to last 2
stitches, K2tog—73 stitches.

Row 1 (Wrong Side): Work in Shaker Rib stitch pattern until work measures 7 inches [18 cm] from cast-on edge, end on a Right Side row.

SHAPE CROWN
Row 1 (Wrong Side): K1 *Sl 1, K2tog, PSSO,
K4. Repeat from * to last 2 sts, K2—53 stitches.
Row 2: K1, *K1-B, P1. Repeat from * to last 2 stitches, K1-B, K1.
Row 3: Knit.
Row 4: K1, *K1-B, P1. Repeat from * to last 2 stitches, K1-B, K1.
Row 5: Knit.
Row 6: K1, *K1-B, P1. Repeat from * to last 2 stitches, K1-B, K1.
Row 7: K1 *Sl 1, K2tog, PSSO, K2. Repeat
from * to last 2 stitches, K2—33 stitches.
Row 8: K1, P1, *K1-B. Repeat from * to last st, K1.
Row 9: Knit.
Rows 10-15: Repeat Rows 8 and 9three times more.
Row 16 (Right Side): K2tog across row to last st, K1—17 stitches.

FINISHING
Cut yarn leaving a tail approximately 15 inches [38 cm] long. With yarn needle, draw tail through remaining stitches twice, fasten securely and sew seam. Weave in ends.

Seed Banded Slouch Hat

Slouch hats are very popular and this is a cute version of this type of hat. It is made with Lion Brand's cashmere yarn for a soft luxurious feel. You can substitute another yarn as long as you use the weight category 3 light worsted yarn in its place.

What You'll Need:

4.4 ounces or 125 grams of light worsted yarn, pattern uses 5 balls of Lion Brand Collection Cashmere in Pewter 483-152
Size 6 double point needles
16 inch size 6 circular needle
Stitch markers and tapestry needle

Gauge for pattern is 19 stitches equal 4 in. (10 cm) in Stocking stitch worked in the round (knit every round) with 2 strands of yarn held together.

HAT
Cast on 88 stitches onto circular needle with 2 strands of yarn held together Place marker for beg of round. Join by knitting the first stitch on the left hand needle with the working yarn from the right hand needle and being careful not to twist stitches.
Rnd 1: Purl.
Rnd 2: Knit.
Rnd 3: Purl.
Rnds 4-7: Knit.
Rep Rnds 1-7 once, then repeat Rounds 1-3 once more.
Next Rnd (Inc):K6, slightly separate the 2 strands of next stitch and k into each strand separately (1 stitch increased), *k8, k into each strand of next stitch separately; repeat from * around - 98 stitches at the end of this rnd.
Work in St stitch worked in the round (k every round) for 8 rounds.

Seed Stitch Band
Rnd 1: Purl.
Rnds 2 and 3: Knit.
Rnd 4: *K1, p1; repeat from * around.
Rnd 5: *P1, k1; repeat from * around.
Rnds 6 and 7: Knit.
Rnds 8 and 9: Repeat Rounds 4 and 5.
Rnds 10 and 11: Knit.
Rnd 12: Purl.
Work in St stitch worked in the round for 13 rounds, then rep Rounds 1-12 of Seed stitch band.
Work in St stitch worked in the round for 11 rounds.
Shape Crown (top of Hat)

Rnds 1 and 3: Purl.
Rnd 2 (Dec): *K12, k2tog;repeat from * around – 91 stitches at the end of this rnd.
Rnds 4-8: Knit.
Rnds 9 and 11: Purl.
Rnd 10 (Dec): *K5, k2tog;repeat from * around – 78 stitches.
Rnds 12-14: Knit.
Rnds 15 and 17: Purl.
Rnd 16 (Dec): *K2, k2tog;repeat from * around to last 2 stitches, k2 – 59 stitches.
Rnds 17-19 18-20: Knit.
Rnd 18 21 (Dec): *K1, k2tog;repeat from * around to last 2 stitches, k2 - 40 stitches.
Rnds 20-22 22-24: Knit.
Rnd 23 25 (Dec): *K2tog;repeat from * around - 20 stitches.

Cut yarn, leaving a long yarn tail.Thread tail through remaining stitches and pull to gather. Knot to secure.

FINISHING
Weave in ends.

Diagonal Stitch Pom-Pom Hat

This is a really cute hat with a diagonal pattern and a sporty pom-pom topping it off. It is sized for an average woman's size head, but you could make is larger or smaller with different size needles.

What You'll Need:

4 ounces or 113 grams of medium weight worsted yarn; pattern uses 1 skein of Caron® United™ Orange (06010)
US size 8 (5mm) knitting needles

Gauge for patterns is 17 stiches and 23 rows equal 4 inches (10 cm) in stocking stitch.

Cast on 78 stitches.
1st row: (WS). Knit.
Proceed in pat as follows:
1st row: (RS). *K3. P2.Repeat from * to last 3 stitches. K3.
2nd row: P2. *K2. P3.Repeat from * to last st. K1.
3rd row: *P2. K3. Repeat from * to last 3 stitches. P2. K1.
4th row: *K2. P3. Repeat from * to last 3 stitches. K2. P1.

5th row: K2. *P2. K3. Repeat from * to last st. P1.
6th row: *P3. K2. Repeat from * to last 3 stitches. P3.
7th row: P1. *K3. P2.Repeat from * to last 2 stitches. K2.
8th row: P1. *K2. P3. Repeat from * to last 2 stitches. K2.
9th row: K1. *P2. K3. Repeat from * to last 2 stitches. P2.
10th row: K1. *P3. K2. Repeat from * to last 2 stitches. P2.
These 10 rows form Diagonal Pattern
Continue in Diagonal Pat until work from beginning measures about 8 inches [20.5 cm], ending on
a 10th row of pattern.
Shape crown: 1st row: (RS). *K1. K2tog.
P2. Repeat from * to last 3 stitches. K1. K2tog. 62 stitches.
2nd row: P1. *K2. P2. Repeat from * to last
st. K1. 3rd row: *P2. K2tog. Repeat from * to last 2 stitches. P2. 47 stitches.
4th row: K1. *P1. K2tog. Repeat from * to last st. P1. 32 stitches.
5th row: *K2tog. Repeat from * end of row.16 stitches.
Break yarn, leaving a long end.
Draw end tightly through rem stitches and fasten securely. Sew center back seam.
Weave in all ends.

Pompom: Wind yarn around 4 fingers about 100 times. Remove from fingers and tightly tie around the
center. Cut through each side of loops. Trim to a smooth round shape. Sew to top of Hat.

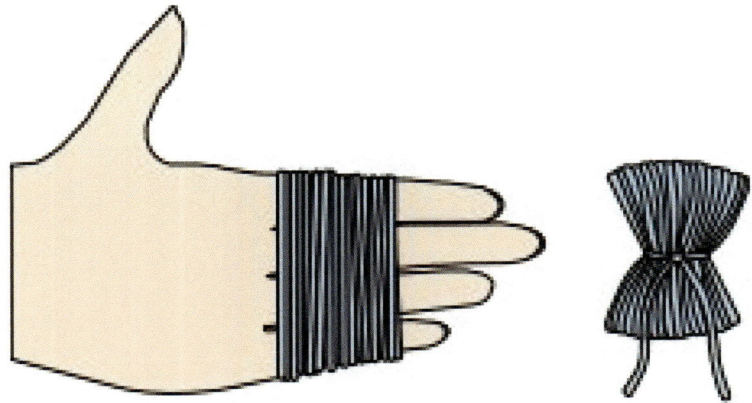

Family Striped Beanies

This pattern has sizes for the entire family plus three different stripe variations. You can knit up a hat for each member of your family and use their favorite colors. Sizes are for children ages 4/6 and 8/10 years, men's and women's.

What You'll Need:

1 4 ounce (113 gram) skein each for Color A, B, and C. Pattern uses Caron Caron® United® Contrast A Navy (06014), Contrast B Aran (06002),and Contrast C Burgundy (06009).
US size 8 or 5mm needle

GAUGE: 17 stitches and 23 rows equal 4inches (10 cm) in stocking stitch

Pattern is written for smallest size with the other sizes in parenthesis. If no other numbers appear the directions are for all sizes.

Version 1: C as Color 1, B as Color 2, A as Color 3.
Version 2: B as Color 1, A as Color 2, C as Color 3.
Version 3: A as Color 1, C as Color 2, B as Color 3.

STRIPE PAT
With Color 2: 4 rows.
With Color 3: 4 rows.
These 8 rows form Stripe Pattern

HAT
With Color 1, cast on 74 (78-82-86) stitches.
Work 6 rows stocking stitch, noting 1st row is RS. Break Color 1.
With Color 3, work in stocking stitch until work from beg (allowing cast on edge to roll) measures approximately2 (2½-3-3½) inches [5 (6-7.5-9) cm], ending on a Wrong Side row.

Work Stripe Pat in stocking stitch until work from beg (allowing cast on edge to roll) measures approximately 5½ (7-8-8 ½) inches [14 (18-20.5-21.5) cm], ending on a WS row.

Continue in Stripe Pattern,
Shape top: 1st row: K1. *K2tog. K14 (15-16-17). ssk. Repeat from * to last st. K1. 66 (70-74-78) stitches.
2nd and alt rows: Purl.
3rd row: K1. *K2tog. K12 (13-14-15). ssk. Repeat from * to last st. K1. 58 (62-66-70) stitches.
5th row: K1. *K2tog. K10 (11-12-13). ssk. Repeat from * to last st. K1. 50 (54-58-62) stitches.
7th row: K1. *K2tog. K8 (9-10-11). ssk. Repeat from * to last st. K1. 42 (46-50-54) stitches.
9th row: K1. *K2tog. K6 (7-8-9). ssk. Repeat from * to last st. K1. 34 (38-42-46) stitches.
11th row: K1. *K2tog. K4 (5-6-7). ssk. Repeat from * to last st. K1. 26 (30-34-38) stitches.
13th row: K1. *K2tog. K2 (3-4-5). ssk. Repeat from * to last st. K1. 18 (22-26-30) stitches.
15th row: K1. *K2tog. Repeat from * to last st. K1.10 (12-14-16) stitches.
Break yarn, leaving a long end. Draw end tightly through rem stitches. Sew back seam.

Crisscross Headband

Headbands are quick and easy gifts to knit up in a hurry. Headbands are also a way to add some style to your look without a lot of effort. Use different colors and variegated yarns to really show your creativity.

What You'll Need:

3.5 ounces or 100 grams of medium weight yarn, pattern uses RED HEART Luster Sheen® in 251 Orange.
US size 5 (3.75mm) needles
1 ¾ inch plastic headband
Cable needle, yarn needle and straight pins

GAUGE: 36 stitches equal 4 inches (10 cm), 40 rows equal 4 inches (10 cm) in cable pattern.
CHECK YOUR GAUGE. Use any size needles to obtain the gauge

Finished Size: 3½ inches (9 cm) wide (at widest point) x 12 inches (30.5 cm) long.

Special Stitches
Cable2 Front —onto cable needle slip next 2 stitches and hold at front of work, K2from the left needle, K2from the cable needle.
Cable 2 Purl Front – Slip next 2 stitches onto cable needle and hold at front of work, P2 from the left needle, P2 from the cable needle.
Cable 2 Back – onto cable needle slip next 2 stitches and hold at back of work, K2 from the left needle, P2 from the cable needle.

NOTES

1. Headband can be worked following chart, or by reading written instructions.
2. Use a dark colored headband for dark colored yarn, or a light colored headband for light colored yarn.

HEADBAND

Cast on 6 sts.
Row 1: Knit across.
Row 2 (Right side): K1, M1, purl across to last st, M1, K1: 8 stitches.
Rows 3-6: Repeat Rows 1 and 2, twice:12 stitches.
Row 7: Knit across.
Row 8: K1, purl across to last st, K1.
Row 9: Knit across.
Row 10: Repeat Row 2: 14 stitches.
Row 11: Knit across.
Row 12: K1, purl across to last st, K1.
Row 13: Knit across.
Row 14: Repeat Row 2: 16 stitches.
Row 15: Knit across.
Row 16: K1, purl across to last st, K1.
Row 17: K2, P2, K8, P2, K2.
Row 18: K1, M1, P1, Cable 2 Purl Front, K4,
Cable 2 Back, P1, M1, K1: 18 stitches.
Row 19: K5, P2, K4, P2, K5.
Row 20: K1, P4, Cable 2 Purl Front, Cable 2 Back, P4, K1.
Row 21: K7, P4, K7.
Row 22: K1, M1, P6, Cable 2 Front, P6, M1,and K1:20 stitches.
Row 23: K8, P4, K8.
Row 24: K1, K5, Cable 2 Back, Cable 2 Purl Front, P5, K1.
Row 25: K6, P2, K4, P2, K6.
Row 26: K1, M1, P3, Cable 2 Back, P4, Cable 2 Purl Front, P3, M1, K1: 22 stitches.
Row 27: K4, P2, K8, P2, K4.
Row 28: K1, P2, Cable 2 Back, P8, Cable 2 Purl Front, P2, K1.
Row 29: K3, P2, K 12, P2, K3.
Row 30: K1, M1, P2, Cable 2 Purl Front, P8,Cable 2 Back, P2, M1, K1: 24 stitches.
Row 31: K6, P2, K8, P2, K6.
Row 32: K1, P5, Cable 2 Purl Front, P4, Cable 2 Back, P5, K1.
Row 33: K8, P2, K4, P2, K8.
Row 34: K1, M1, P7, Cable 2 Purl Front, Cable 2 Back, P7, M1, K1: 26 stitches.
Row 35: K 11, P4, knit across.
Row 36: K1, P 10, Cable 2 Front, P 10, K1.
Row 37: K 11, P4, knit across.
Row 38: K1, M1, P8, Cable 2 Back, Cable 2 Purl Front, P8, M1, K1: 28 stitches.
Row 39: K 10, P2, K4, P2, knit across.
Row 40: K1, P7, Cable 2 Back, P4, Cable 2 Purl Front, P7, K1.
Row 41: K8, P2, K8, P2, K8.
Row 42: K1, M1, P5, Cable 2 Back, P8, Cable 2 Purl Front, P5, M1, K1: 30 stitches.
Row 43: K7, P2, K 12, P2, K7.
Row 44: K1, P4, Cable 2 Back, P 12, Cable 2 Purl Front, P4, K1.
Row 45: K5, P2, K 14, P2, K5.

Row 46: K1, M1, P2, Cable 2 Purl Front, P 16, Cable 2 Back, P2, M1, K1: 32 stitches.
Row 47: K4, P2, K 20, P2, K4.
Row 48: K1, P3, Cable 2 Purl Front, P 16, Cable 2 Back, P3, K1.
Row 49: K6, P2, K 16, P2, K6.
Row 50: K1, P5, Cable 2 Purl Front, P 12, Cable 2 Back, P5, K1.
Row 51: K8, P2, K 12, P2, K8.
Row 52: K1, P7, Cable 2 Purl Front, P8, Cable 2 Back, P7, K1.
Row 53: K 10, P2, K8, P2, knit across.
Row 54: K1, P9, Cable 2 Purl Front, P4, Cable 2 Back, P9, K1.
Row 55: K 12, P2, K4, P2, knit across.
Row 56: K1, P 11, Cable 2 Purl Front, Cable 2 Back, P 11, K1.
Row 57: K 14, P4, knit across.
Row 58: K1, P 13, Cable 2 Front, P 13, K1.
Row 59: K 14, P4, knit across.
Row 60: K1, P 11, Cable 2 Back, Cable 2 Purl Front, P 11, K1.
Row 61: K 12, P2, K4, P2, knit across.
Row 62: K1, P9, Cable 2 Back, P4, Cable 2 Purl Front, P9, K1.
Row 63: K 10, P2, K8, P2, knit across.
Row 64: K1, P7, Cable 2 Back, P8, Cable 2 Purl Front, P7, K1.
Row 65: K8, P2, K 12, P2, K8.
Row 66: K1, P5, Cable 2 Back, P 12, Cable 2 Purl Front, P5, K1.
Row 67: K6, P2, K 16, P2, K6.
Row 68: K1, P3, Cable 2 Back, P 16, Cable 2 Purl Front, P3, K1.
Row 69: K4, P2, K 20, P2, K4.
Row 70: K1, K2tog, P1, Cable 2 Purl Front, P 16, Cable 2 Back, P1, SSK, K1: 30 stitches.
Row 71: K5, P2, K 14, P2, K5.
Row 72: K1, P4, Cable 2 Purl Front, P 12, Cable 2 Back, P4, K1.
Row 73: K7, P2, K 12, P2, K7.
Row 74: K1, K2tog, P4, Cable 2 Purl Front, P8, Cable 2 Back, P4, SSK, K1: 28 stitches.
Row 75: K8, P2, K8, P2, K8.
Row 76: K1, P7, Cable 2 Purl Front, P4, Cable 2 Back, P7, K1.
Row 77: K 10, P2, K4, P2, knit across.
Row 78: K1, K2tog, P7, Cable 2 Purl Front, Cable 2 Back, P7, SSK, K1: 26 stitches.
Row 79: K 11, P4, knit across.
Row 80: K1, P 10, Cable 2 Front, P 10, K1.
Row 81: K 11, P4, knit across.
Row 82: K1, K2tog, P6, Cable 2 Back, Cable 2 Purl Front, P6, SSK, K1: 24 stitches.
Row 83: K8, P2, K4, P2, K8.
Row 84: K1, P5, Cable 2 Back, P4, Cable 2 Purl Front, P5, K1.
Row 85: K6, P2, K8, P2, K6.
Row 86: K1, K2tog, P1, Cable 2 Back, P8, Cable 2 Purl Front, P1, SSK, K1: 22 stitches.
Row 87: K3, P2, K 12, P2, K3.
Row 88: K1, P2, Cable 2 Purl Front, P8, Cable 2 Back, P2, K1.
Row 89: K4, P2, K8, P2, K4.
Row 90: K1, K2tog, P2, Cable 2 Purl Front, P4, Cable 2 Back, P2, SSK, K1: 20 stitches.
Row 91: K6, P2, K4, P2, K6.
Row 92: K1, P5, Cable 2 Purl Front, Cable 2 Back, P5, K1.
Row 93: K8, P4, K8.
Row 94: K1, K2tog, P5, Cable 2 Front, P5, SSK, K1: 18 stitches.
Row 95: K7, P4, K7.

Row 96: K1, P4, Cable 2 Back, Cable 2 Purl Front, P4, K1.
Row 97: K5, P2, K4, P2, K5.
Row 98: K1, K2tog, Cable 2 Back, K4, Cable 2 Purl Front, SSK, K1: 16 stitches.
Row 99: K2, P2, K8, P2, K2.
Row 100: K1, purl across to last st, K1.
Row 101: Knit across.
Row 102: K1, K2tog, purl across to last 3 stitches, SSK, K1: 14 stitches.
Row 103: Knit across.
Row 104: K1, purl across to last st, K1.
Row 105: Knit across.
Row 106: K1, K2tog, purl across to last 3 stitches,
SSK, K1: 12 stitches.
Rows 107–110: Repeat Rows 103–106—10 stitches.
Row 111: Knit across.
Row 112: K1, K2tog, purl across to last 3 stitches, SSK, K1: 8 stitches.
Row 113: Knit across.
Row 114: K1, K2tog, purl across to last 3 stitches, SSK, K1: 6 stitches.
Row 115: Knit across.
Bind off all stitches in knit, leaving a long end for sewing.

FINISHING
Thread a yarn needle with the long end. With right side facing, wrap Headband around plastic headband and pin in place. Sew side seams and edges together, matching ends of rows and stitches.

Pattern Chart

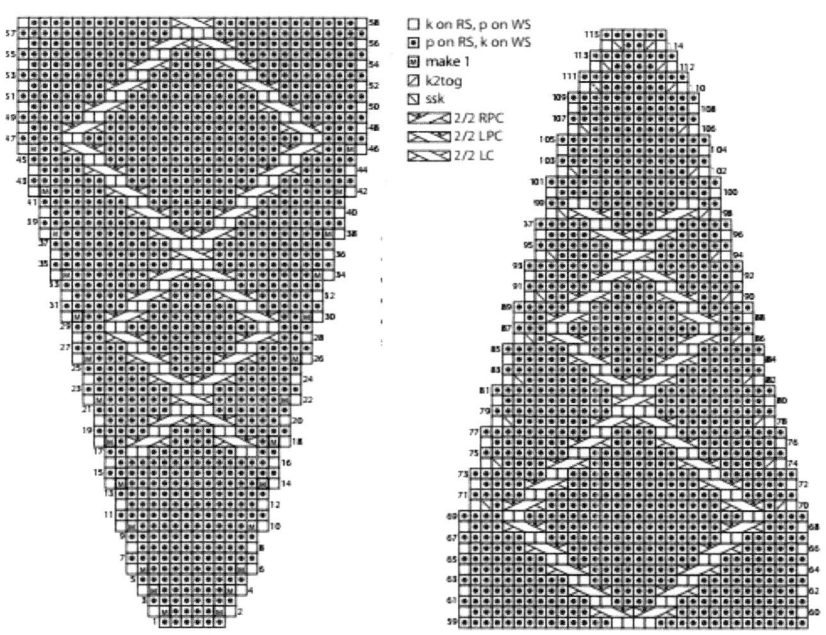

- ☐ k on RS, p on WS
- ⊡ p on RS, k on WS
- ☑ make 1
- ⧄ k2tog
- ⧅ ssk
- ⬚ 2/2 RPC
- ⬚ 2/2 LPC
- ⬚ 2/2 LC

Garter Stitch Hat

This hat is actually two squares knitted in the garter stitch and then sewn together. The alternating stripes created by the stitches and yarn make this a truly unique and beautiful hat. This hat was designed by Bobby Fitzgerald for Lion Brand Yarns.

What You'll Need:

Pattern is worked in 671-150 Lion's Pride Woolspun: Oxford Grey (A) and 671-149 Lion's Pride Woolspun: Charcoal(B)
Size 10.5 (6.5mm) needles and a tapestry needle

NOTES:
1. Two Squares are worked in easy Garter stitch (knit every stitch on every row) and stripes.
2. Squares are sewn together, and one edge is gathered to make hat.

STEP 1
Square 1
Cast on 28 stitches with A,.

STEP 2
Knit with A for 6 rows.
*With B knit for 4 rows; with A, knit for 4 rows; repeat from * 5 more times; then with B, knit for 4 rows.

Bind off.

STEP 3
Square 2
With B, cast on 28 stitches.
With B, work in Garter stitch for 4 rows.
*With A, knit 2 rows; with B, knit 2 rows; repeat from * 11 more times; with A, work in Garter stitch for 4 rows.
Bind off.

STEP 4
Sew Squares together.

STEP 5
Thread needle with a length of either color yarn and weave in and out of one edge of Hat.

STEP 6
Pull yarn to gather, then knot to secure.
Weave in yarn ends.

Finished Circumference About 19 in. (48.5 cm), stretches to fit

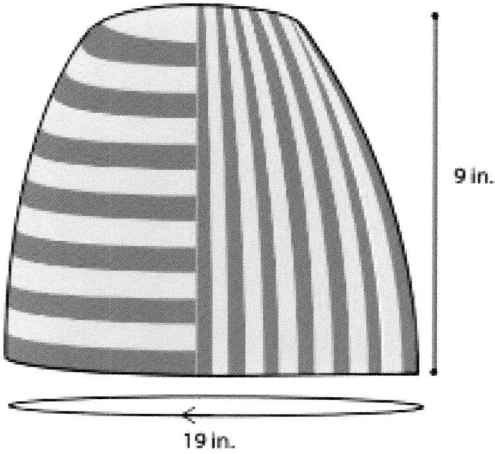

9 in.

19 in.

Thread needle with a length of either color yarn and weave in and out of one edge of Hat.

Pull yarn to gather, then knot to secure.
Weave in yarn ends.

Romancing the Hat

How cute is this hat and how colorful? You can really feel the love when you put this hat on. Make it for Valentine's Day or for whenever you need some bright cheery colors in your life.

What You'll Need:

Pattern is made with Red Heart With Love™: One skein each:
1252 Mango A
1909 Holly Berry B
1703 Candy Pink C
1538 Lilac D
US size 9 (5.5mm) needles, optional pompom maker

Finished Measurements: 17 (18¾, 20½) inches
GAUGE: 14 stitches equal 4inches; 32 rows equal 4 inches in pattern.

Hat
With A, cast on 62(68, 74) sts.
Row 1 (Right Side): Knit.
Row 2: P1, knit to last st, p1.
Repeat Rows 1 and 2 for 1 inches, end Row 2.Change to B and work in pattern as follows:
Rows 1 and 3 (RS): Knit.
Row 2: Purl.
Row 4: P1, knit to last st, p1.

Row 5:K1, purl to last st, k1.
Row 6: P1, knit to last st, p1.
Rows 1-6 form pattern. Repeat Rows 1-6 with C, then D, A, and B. Continue in this sequence until hat measures 7 (8, 9) inches from beginning, end Row 6.

Shape Crown
Keeping continuity of color sequence, work as follows:
Row 1 (Right Side): K1, [k8 (9, 10), k2tog] 6 times, k1 – 56 (62, 68) stitches.
Row 2: Purl 1 row even.
Row 3: K1, [k7 (8, 9), k2tog] 6 times, k1 – 50 (56, 62) stitches.
Row 4: P1, knit to last st, p1.
Row 5: K1, [p6 (7, 8), p2tog] 6 times, k1 – 44 (50, 56) stitches.
Row 6: Repeat Row 4.
Row 7: K1, [k5 (6, 7), k2tog] 6 times, k1 – 38 (44, 50) stitches.
Row 8: Repeat Row 2.
Row 9: K1, [k4 (5, 6), k2tog] 6 times, k1 – 32 (38, 44) stitches.
Row 10: Repeat Row 4.
Row 11: K1, [p3 (4, 5), p2tog] 6 times, k1 – 26 (32, 38) stitches.
Row 12: Repeat Row 4.
Row 13: K1, [k2 (3, 4), k2tog] 6 times, k1 – 20 (26, 32) stitches.
Row 14: Repeat Row 2.
Row 15: K1, [k1 (2, 3), k2tog] 6 times, k1 – 14 (20, 26) stitches.
Row 16: Repeat Row 4.
Row 17: K1, [p0 (1, 2), p2tog] 6 times, k1 – 8 (14, 20) stitches.

Sizes Medium and Large Only-Row 18: Repeat Row 4.
Row 19: K1, [p (0, 1), p2tog] 6 times, k1 – 8 (14) stitches.

Size Large Only-Row 20: Repeat Row 2.
Row 21: K1, [p2tog] 6 times, k1 – 8 stitches.

All Sizes
Cut yarn leaving a 15 inches tail. With tail in yarn needle, weave through remaining stitches, draw up and fasten securely and then sew back seam.

Chapter Six – Knitting for Baby

In this chapter I will share some of the cutest baby patterns I've found for free on the internet. When possible I gave credit to the original designer. Baby items are fun to knit, and what is cuter than a baby in a homemade outfit snuggled up in a hand knitted Afghan? Not much! I've included a variety of baby items for you to knit in this chapter from hats, garments, Afghans, and accessories.

Bernat Baby Coordinates Afghan

This super cute baby Afghan knits up quickly and has a light lacey feel. You can make this any color for a boy or a girl, or if you don't know use a neutral color. The aqua shown in the picture would be perfect for a little boy or little girl.

What You'll Need:

5 ball of 5.6 ounce or 160 gram balls of baby weight yarn. The pattern uses 5 balls of Bernat Baby Coordinates
US size 7 (4.5mm) 32 inch circular needles

Gauge is 24 stitches and 28 rows equal 3 inches

yfwd. Equals yarn forward

INSTRUCTIONS
Cast on 217 stitches. Knit 6 rows.

Proceed in pat as follows:
1st row: (RS). K4. *yfwd. K3. Sl1K. K2tog. psso. K3. yfwd. K1. Rep from * to last 3 sts. K3.
2nd row: K3.Purl to last 3 stitches. K3.
3rd row: As 1st row.
4th row: Knit.
These4 rows form pattern.
Continue in pattern until work from beg measures approximately 45 ins [114.5 cm], ending with 2nd row of pattern.
Knit 6 rows. Cast off knit wise.

Baby Love Diagonal Baby Afghan

This baby Afghan is knitted on large circular needles to hold the number of stitches, but it is knit back and forth like you were working with straight needles. You start with a small number of stitches and work up to 207 and then start to decrease.

What You'll Need

Pattern is made with 1 ball Lion Brand's Pound of Love worsted weight yarn in Antique White. You can use any 4 weight worsted yarn you want if you prefer.
24 inch US size 8 circular needle
Tapestry needle

Gauge 19 stitches equal 4 inches [10 cm] in garter stitch (knit every row).

BLANKET
Cast on 5 stitches.
Row 1: Knit.
Row 2: K 3, yo, k 2.
Row 3: K 3, yo, k 3.
Row 4: K 3, yo,knit to end of row.
Repeat last row until you have 207stitches on needle.
Next (decrease) row: K 2, k2 tog, yo, k2 tog, k to end of row.
Repeat last row until 5 sts remain. Bind off.
FINISHING
Weave in ends.

Baby Swing Coat

Your little girl or granddaughter will be right in style in the super cute baby swing coat designed by Kristin Omdahl for Red Heart. Made with bulky yarn it works up fast and is very soft and warm. Pattern is written for 12 months. Changes for sizes 18 months and 24 months are in parentheses.

What You'll Need:

5.25 or 7.04 ounces (150 or 200 grams) or bulky weight baby yarn. Patter uses 3 (3. 4) BALLS OF RED HEART Buttercup® in 4930 Cutie Pie.
US size 11 (8mm) 29 inch circular needle
US size H-8 (5mm) crochet hook for button loop
Stitch holder, one 1 ½ inch (4cm) button
Sewing thread, needle, and yarn needle

GAUGE: 10 stitches equal 4 inches (10 cm); 14 rows equal 4inches (10 cm)

Finished Chest: 25 (26, 27) inches (63.5 (66, 68.5) cm)
Finished Length: 14¼, (14¾, 15) inches (36 (37.5, 38) cm)

BODY
Loosely cast on 93 (97, 102) stitches
Knit 4 rows.
Row 1 (right side): Knit.
Row 2: K1, purl to last st, k1.
Repeat last 2 rows until piece measures about 9 inches (23 cm) from beginning; end with a wrong side row.
Decrease Row (right side):K0 (1, 0), *k2tog, k1; repeat from * to end of row—62 (65, 68) stitches.
Next Row: K1, purl to last st, k1.
Divide at Underarms (RS): K15 (16, 17) for right front, bind off 1 st, k30 (31, 32) for back, bind off 1 st, k15 (16, 17) for left front.

Left Front
Row 1 (wrong side): K1, p14 (15, 16); place remaining stitches on holder—15 (16, 17) stitches.
Row 2:Ssk, knit to end of row—14 (15, 16) stitches.
Row 3:K1, purl to end of row.
Row 4:Knit to last 2 stitches, k2tog—13 (14, 15) stitches.
Row 5: K1, purl to end of row.
Rows 6–11:Repeat last 2 rows 3 more times—10 (11, 12) stitches at the end of Row 11.
Row 12: Knit.
Row 13: K1, purl to end of row.
Rows 14–17 (17, 19): Repeat last 2 rows 2 (2, 3) more times.
Size 18 months only: Repeat Row 12.
Bind off.

Back
Return the 30 (31, 32) back stitches from holder to needle, ready to work a wrong side row.
Row 1 (wrong side): Purl.
Row 2:Ssk, knit to last 2 stitches, k2tog—28 (29, 30) stitches.
Rows 3–17 (18, 19): Beginning with a wrong side (purl) row, work in Stockinette st for 15 (16, 17) rows.
Bind off.
Right Front
Return the 15 (16, 17) right front stitches from holder to needle, ready to work a wrong side row.
Row 1 (wrong side): Purl to last st, k1.
Row 2: Knit to last 2 stitches, k2tog—14 (15, 16) stitches.

Row 3: Purl to last st, k1.
Row 4:Ssk, knit to end of row—13 (14, 15) stitches.
Row 5: Purl to last st, k1.
Rows 6–11: Repeat last 2 rows 3 more times—10 (11, 12) stitches at the end of Row 11.
Row 12: Knit.
Row 13: Purl to last st, k1.
Rows 14–17 (17, 19): Repeat last 2 rows 2 (2, 3) more times.
Size 18 months only: Repeat Row 12.
Bind off.
Sew shoulder seams.

SLEEVES (work 2)
Row 1 (right side): With RS facing, beginning and ending at underarm, pick up and knit 24 (26, 28) stitches evenly spaced across armhole edge.
Rows 2–10 (12, 14): Beginning with a WS row, work in Stockinette stitch for 9 (11, 13) rows.
Row 11 (13, 15): Ssk, knit to last 2 stitches, k2tog—22 (24, 26) stitches.
Row 12 (14, 16): Purl.
Rows 13 (15, 17)–18 (20, 22): Repeat last 2 rows 3 more times—16 (18, 20) stitches.
Rows 19 (21, 23)–23 (25, 27): Knit 5 rows.
Bind off. Cut yarn, leaving a long tail for sewing sleeve seam.
FINISHING
Sew sleeve seams.

Button Loop
With RS facing use a crochet hook and join yarn with slip stitch in the corner of right neck, chain 5, slip stitch in front edge about 1 inch below joining slip stitch. Fasten off.
Sew button to left front on the opposite side of the button loop.
Weave in ends.

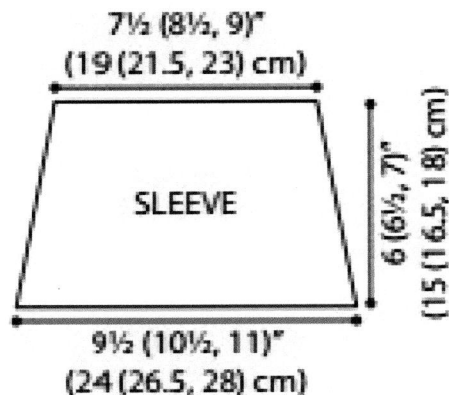

7½ (8½, 9)"
(19 (21.5, 23) cm)

SLEEVE

6 (6½, 7)"
(15 (16.5, 18) cm)

9½ (10½, 11)"
(24 (26.5, 28) cm)

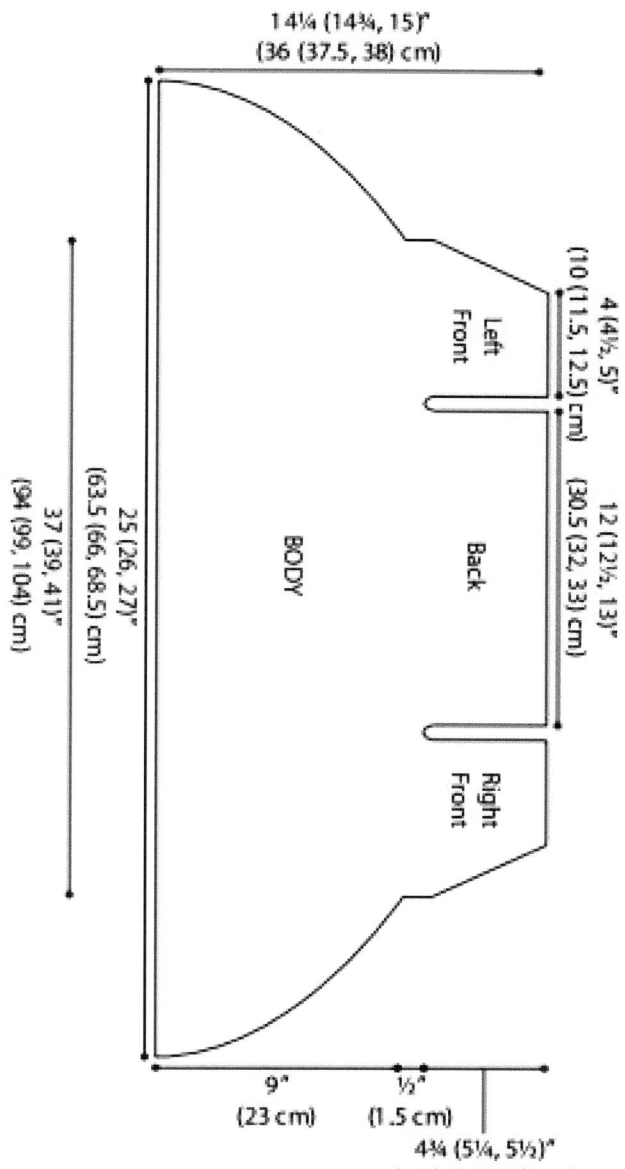

14¼ (14¾, 15)"
(36 (37.5, 38) cm)

4 (4½, 5)"
(10 (11.5, 12.5) cm)

Left
Front

Back

12 (12½, 13)"
(30.5 (32, 33) cm)

BODY

Right
Front

25 (26, 27)"
(63.5 (66, 68.5) cm)

37 (39, 41)"
(94 (99, 104) cm)

9"
(23 cm)

½"
(1.5 cm)

4¾ (5¼, 5½)"
(12 (13.5, 14) cm)

Mixed Baby Stripe Throw

Although this pattern is knitted in green and blue you can change the color to match baby's nursery. The yarn used for this throw is a cotton hemp blend which makes the throw lightweight yet warm enough for even cold nights. The throw was designed by Martha Stewart for Lion Brand Yarns.

What you'll need:

3 balls each of Martha Stewart Crafts TM/MC Cotton Hemp Yarn in the following colors:
5700-506 Blue Icing Color A
5700-500 Flour Sack White Color B
5700-530 Picnic Green Color C
5700-578 Peacock Color D

29 inch size 7 circular needle
Split ring stitch markers and tapestry needle

GAUGE:
17 stitches equal 4 inches (10 cm) in Stockinette stitch (k on RS, p on WS).

THROW

With A, cast on 120 stitches.

Rows 1-10: Work in Seed st.

Row 11 (RS):With A, work in Seed stitch as established over first 7 stitches for border, place marker (pm), k to last 7 stitches, pm, work in Seed stitch as established over last 7 stitches for border.

Row 12:With A, work in Seed stitch as established over first 7 stitches, slip marker (sm), purl to last 7 stitches, sm, work in Seed stitch as established over last 7 stitches.

Continue as established, working stitches outside of markers (the first and last 7 stitches) in Seed stitch, the remaining stitches in Stockinette stitch (k on RS, p on WS), changing color as follows:

Rows 13 and 14: With A.

Rows 15-18: With B.

Rows 19-38: With C.

Rows 39 and 40: With D.

Rows 41-46: With B.

Rows 47-58: With A.

Rows 59-64: With D.

Rows 65-66: With C.

Rows 67-80: With B.

Rows 81-84: With A.

Rows 85–92: With D.

Rows 93–100: With C.

Rows 101 and 102: With B.

Rows 103–118: With A.

Rows 119–122: With C.

Rows 123–140: With D.

Rows 141–148: With B.

Rows 149-152: With A.

Rows 153-168: With C.

Row 169: With D.

Row 170:Rep Row 169, removing markers as you come to them.

Rows 171-180:With B, work in Seed stitch.

Bind off.

FINISHING

Weave in ends.

Feather and Fan Baby Blanket

This is another baby blanket sure to become a favorite of mother and baby alike. The feather and fan pattern makes a very pretty stitch combination. You can switch up the colors to match baby's room in this blanket, too.

What You'll Need:

1 ball each of Bernat® Baby Sport Solid Yarn
Color A #21005 Baby White
Color B #21302 Baby Denim Marl

Or you can use Bernat® Baby Sport Ombres 2 balls each for Color A and Color B
36 inch US 6 (4mm) circular needle

GAUGE
22 stitches and 30 rows equal 4 inches (10 cm) in stocking stitch.

MEASUREMENTS
Approximately 37 x 44 inches (94 x 112 cm)

ABBREVIATIONS
K1B equal Knit into next stitch 1 row below

INSTRUCTIONS
With A, cast on 224 stitches. Do not join in rnd.
Bottom edging: Work back and forth across needle, knit 7 rows (garter stitch), noting 1st row is WS.

Proceed in pat as follows:

1st row: (RS). With MC, K4. *(K1B. K1) 9 times. yfwd. K4. Sl1. K1.psso. K6. K2tog. K4. yfwd. Rep from * 5 times more. K4.

2nd row: K4. *P1. yrn. P4. P2tog. P4. P2togtbl. P4. yrn. P1. (P1. K1) 9 times. Rep from * 5 times more. K4.

3rd row: K4. *(K1B. K1) 9 times. K2. yfwd. K4. Sl1. K1. psso. K2.K2tog. K4. yfwd. K2. Rep from * 5 times more. K4.

4th row: K4. *P3. yrn. P4. P2tog. P2togtbl. P4. yrn. P3. (P1. K1) 9 times. Rep from * 5 times more. K4.

5th to 16th rows: As 1st to 4th rows 3 times more. Break MC.

17th row: With A, K4. *yfwd. K4. Sl1. K1. psso. K6. K2tog. K4. yfwd. (K1B. K1) 9 times. Rep from * 5 times more. K4.

18th row: K4. *(P1. K1) 9 times. P1. yrn. P4. P2tog. P4. P2togtbl. P4. yrn. P1. Rep from * 5 times more. K4.

19th row: K4. *K2. yfwd. K4. Sl1. K1. psso. K2. K2tog. K4. yfwd. K2. (K1B. K1) 9 times. Rep from * 5 times more. K4.

20th row: K4. *(P1. K1) 9 times. P3. yrn. P4. P2tog. P2togtbl. P4. yrn. P3. Rep from * 5 times more. K4.

21st to 32nd rows: As 17th to 20th rows 3 times more. Break A.

Rep 1st to 32nd rows until work from beg measures approx. 43 ins [109 cm], ending with 16th row of pattern.

Top edging: With A, knit7 rows. Cast off knit wise (WS).

Knit Shell Bunting

Buntings and cocoons keep baby warm and snug. The front of the bunting unbuttons for easy changing. The yarn called for in the pattern is discontinued on the Lion Brand site, but you can use any 2 weight sport baby yarn to knit this pattern.

What You'll Need:

1 ball each of 1.75 ounce (50 gram) solid and print or variegated yarn.
Size 4 (3.5mm) and size 6 (4mm) needle
6 buttons and a tapestry needle

GAUGE:
21 stitches equal 4 inches and 36 rows equal 4inches (10 cm)

STITCH EXPLANATION:
PATTERN STITCH (multiple of 9 sts plus 3)
Note Original number of stitches increase from Row 1 and is restored in Row 7.
Row 1 (RS) K2, * yo, k8, yo, k1; rep from * , end last rep k2 instead of k1.
Row 2 K3, * p8, k3;repeat from * to end.
Row 3 K3, * yo, k8, yo, k3; rep from * to end.
Row 4 K4, * p8, k5; rep from * , end last rep k4.
Row 5 K4, * yo, k8, yo, k5; rep from *, end last rep k4.
Row 6 K5, * p8, k7; rep from * , end last rep k5.
Row 7 K5, * k4 tog thru back lps, k4 tog, k7; rep from * , end last rep k5.
Row 8 Knit. Rep Rows 1 - 8 for pat st.

BUNTING
BACK
With larger needles and CC, cast on 75 stitches. Work in garter stitch (knit every row) for 8 rows.
Continue in pattern as follows: * With MC, work Rows 1 - 8 of pat stitch twice; with CC, work Rows 1 - 8 of pattern stitch once; repeat from * (24 rows) 4 times more. With MC, work Rows 1 - 8 of past stitch twice—piece measures approximately 16 inches from beginning .With CC, k next row, decrease 12 stitches evenly spaced across—63 stitches. With CC, work in garter stitch for 5 rows more.
Shape Armhole Continue in garter stitch with CC, bind off 3 stitches at beg of next 2 rows—57 stitches. Work 24 rows of pattern stitch as before once more, then with MC, work Rows 1 - 8 of pattern stitch twice.
Shape Shoulder With MC, knit, binding off 18 stitches at beg of next 2 rows. Bind off remaining 21 stitches for back neck.

LEFT FRONT
With larger needles and CC, cast on 39 .Work in garter stitch for 8 rows. Work 24 rows of pattern stitch same as back until piece measures 16 inches from beg.
Next Row (RS) With CC, knit, decrease 6 stitches evenly spaced across—33 stitches. Continue in garter stitch for 5 rows more.
Shape Armhole: Next Row (RS) Bind off 3 stitches, k to end—30 stitches. K 1 row with CC. Work 24 rows of pat stitch once, then with MC work Rows 1 - 7 of pat stitch.
Shape Neck: Next Row (WS) With MC, bind off 9stitches at beg of row(neck edge), k to end. Continue in pat same as back, decrease 1 stitch at neck edge every other row 3times—18 stitches. Work even until same length as back. Bind off stitches for shoulder.

RIGHT FRONT
Work to correspond to left front, reversing all shaping.

SLEEVES

With smaller needles and CC, cast on 27 stitches. Work in k1, p1 ribbing for 6 rows, increase 3 stitches evenly spaced across last row—30 stitches. Change to larger needles. Work in pat stitch same as back, increase 1 stitch each side decrease (working increase stitch in garter stitch) every 4th row 8 times—46 stitches. Work even until piece measures 5 inches from beginning. Bind off.

FINISHING
Sew shoulder seams.
Neckband With Right Side facing and with smaller needles and CC, begin at right front edge, pick up and knit 51stitches around the neck edge. Work in k1, p1 ribbing for 6 rows. Bind off in ribbing.
Left Front Band With larger needles and CC, beginning at top of left front, pick up and k97stitches along left front edge. Work in garter stitch for 8 rows. Bind off. Place markers on band for 6 buttons, first marker ¾ inches from top edge, last marker ¾ inches from lower edge, others spaced evenly between.
Right Front Band:
Work same as left front band for 3 rows. Work buttonholes opposite markers on next row by binding off 2 stitches for each buttonhole. Knit next row, cast on 2 stitches over each set of bound-off stitches. Knit 3 rows more. Bind off. Place stitch markers on the front and the back four inches down from shoulder seam. Sew top of sleeve to front and back between markers. Sew side and sleeve seams. Sew on buttons.

Bunny Pillow Pal

This is a very cute stuffed animal you can make for a toddler. It will be a favorite lovey for many years. The pattern was designed by Nancy Anderson for Red Heart. When finished the pillow measures about 21 inches high by 19 inches wide.

What You'll Need:

1 skein each of RED HEART Super Saver®
373 Petal Pink for Color A
722 Pretty 'N Pink for Color B

US size 11 (8mm) straight needles and double point needles
24 inch US size 11 (8mm) circular needle
Yarn needle, stitch marker, soft standard pillow, 2-1 ½ inch buttons, Velcro hook and loop fastener, stuffing, a sewing needle and matching thread

GAUGE: 12 stitches equal 4 inches; 16 rows equal 4 inches in Stockinette stitch with double Strands of yarn.

Pillow Pal
Head
Using A held double and double pointed needles, cast on 6 stitches; join to work in a circle being careful not to twist stitches.
Round 1: [Increase]6 times – 12 stitches.
Round 2: [K1, increase]6 times – 18 stitches.
Round 3: [K2, increase]6 times – 24 stitches.
Round 4: [K3, increase]6 times – 30 stitches.
Round 5: [K4, increase]6 times – 36 stitches.
Round 6: [K5, increase]6 times – 42 stitches.
Round 7: [K6, increase]6 times – 48 stitches.
Round 8: [K7, increase]6 times – 54 stitches.
Round 9: [K8, increase]6 times – 60 stitches.
Rounds 10-18: Knit.
Round 19: [K8, decrease] 6 times – 54 stitches.
Round 20: [K7, decrease] 6 times – 48 stitches.
Round 21: [K6, decrease] 6 times – 42 stitches.
Rounds 22-37: Knit.
Round 38: [K5, decrease] 6 times – 36 stitches.
Round 39: [K4, decrease] 6 times – 30 stitches.
Round 40: [K3, decrease] 6 times – 24 stitches.
Round 41: [K2, decrease] 6 times – 18 stitches.
Stuff head firmly.

Round 41: [K1, decrease] 6 times – 12 sts.
Finish stuffing. Bind off. Weave yarn tail through stitches to close hole.

Ears (Make 2)
Using A held double and knitting needles, cast on 3 stitches.
Rows 1, 3, 5: Purl.
Row 2: [Increase]3 times – 6 stitches.
Row 4: [Increase] twice, K2, [increase] twice – 10 stitches.
Row 6:Increase, K8, increase – 12 stitches.
Rows 7-13:Work even in St st, end Purl row.
Row 14:Ssk, K8, decrease – 10 stitches.
Rows 15-21: Work even in St st, end Purl row.
Row 22:Ssk, K6, decrease – 8 stitches.
Row 23: Purl.
Bind off, leaving long tail for sewing.

Inner Ear (Make 2)
Using B held double and knitting needles, cast on 2 stitches.
Rows 1, 3, 5: Purl.
Row 2: [Increase] twice – 4 stitches.
Row 4: [Increase]4 times – 8 stitches.
Row 6:Increase, K6, increase – 10 stitches.
Rows 7-13: Work even in St stitch, end Purl row.
Row 14: Ssk, K6, decrease – 8 stitches.
Rows 15-21: Work even in St st, end Purl row.
Row 22:Ssk, K4, decrease – 6 stitches.
Row 23: Purl.
Bind off, leaving long tail for sewing.

Pillow Cover
Using A held double and circular knitting needle, cast on 92stitches.Join to work in the round taking care
that stitches are not twisted. Knit 82 rounds. Bind off.

Closing Strap
Using A cast on 18 stitches onto double and knitting needles,.
Knit 10 rows. Bind off and leave long tail for attaching to pillow cover.

Finishing
With WS together, pin inner ear to outer ear. Sew together and sew the ears to top of the head as
pictured. Pinch them together at the base to form fold.

Onto the face as pictured, sew on buttons . Embroider nose with Satin stitch using B. After you sew the
end seam of the pillow cover closed. Insert the pillow and close the opposite seam.

Locate the midpoint along the short sides of the rectangular pillow,. Pin the closing strap at this
midpoint and attach securely using yarn tail. On the opposite side sew a 2 nch wide piece of loop side
Velcro to the pillow cover using matching thread and a sewing needle. Sew the hook side of the Velcro
along the end of the strap.

Attach the head securely using yarn and a yarn needle working along the longer side of the rectangular pillow, locate the midpoint of the pillow and.

Fair Isle Baby Hat

Fair Isle is a technique used to create lovely designs in knitting projects. You carry the thread across the back of your work twisting the yarn as you pull it forward to work with. This cute baby hat can be made in any color combination to match baby's winter ensemble. The yarn is held double throughout the hat. Pattern fits from 6 to 18 months.

What You'll Need:

Pattern is shown in Red Heart inches Designer Sport™ inches: 1 Ball each 3261 Terra Cotta CA and 3570 Iced Violet CB but these yarns have been discontinued by Red Heart. Any sport weight baby yarn will work for this pattern.
US size 9 (5.5mm) needles
Yarn needle

GAUGE: 18 stitches equal 4 inches and 20 rows equal 4inches in Stockinette stitch using yarn double.

Cast on 72 stitches with CA. Work in K2, P2 ribbing for 10 rows, marking the first row as the RS.

Knit 2 rows with CB. Change to CA and Knit 1 row; Purl 1 row.
Continue in St stitch and work Rows 1- using the Chart. Carry the colors across the WS, changing colors as required and picking up next color to be used under color just used to prevent a hole.

X = CB

	X					
X	X	X				
	X					
					X	
				X	X	X
					X	

With **CA**, Purl 1 row, Knit 1 row. Change to **CB** and Knit 2 rows. Change to **CA** and Purl 1 row.

Shape Crown-Row 1: [K7, K2tog]8 times – 64 stitches.
Row 2 AND ALL WS ROWS: Purl.
Row 3: [K6, K2tog]8 times – 56 stitches.
Row 5: [K5, K2tog]8 times – 48 stitches.
Row 7: [K4, K2tog]8 times – 40 stitches.
Row 9: [K3, K2tog]8 times – 32 stitches.
Row 11: [K2, K2tog]8 times – 24 stitches.
Row 13: [Slip 1, K2tog, psso] 8 times – 8 stitches. Cut yarn leaving a long tail.
With tail in yarn needle, weave through remaining stitches; draw up firmly, fasten securely. Sew back seam. Weave in ends.

Panda Bear Hat

How cute is this hat? I've included this pattern as more of a challenge for you to help you stretch your skills. Don't be intimidated by it though, it's really quite simple if you take it step by step. The Lion Brand Suede yarn has been discontinued, but you can substitute a wool blend or 4 weight baby yarn.

What You'll Need:

1 3 ounce ball of yarn in each color:
Color A – Ecru
Color B – Ebony
Color C – Scarlet (you only need a small amount of red yarn, you don't need an entire ball)
Size 9 (5.5mm) needles
Yarn needle
2 5/8 inch squiggle eyes and fabric glue

GAUGE:
12 stitches plus 19 rows equal 4 inches (10 cm) in Stockinettete stitch (k on RS, p on WS) with A on largest needles.

PANDA HAT
With A,cast on 56(62, 66) sts.Work in St stitch for 22 (24, 26) rows.

Shape Top

Row 1 (RS) K 1 (1, 0), *k 4, k2tog; rep from * 8 (9, 10) times, end k 1 (1 ,0) – 47 (52, 55) stitches.

Rows 2, 4 and 6 Purl.

Row 3 K 1 (1, 0), *k 3, k2tog; rep from * 8 (9, 10) times, end k 1 (1, 0) – 38 (42, 44) stitches.

Row 5 K 1 (1, 0), *k 2, k2tog; rep from * 8 (9,10) times, end k 1 (1, 0) – 29 (32, 33) stitches.

Row 7 K 1 (0, 1), *k2tog; rep from * 13 (15, 15) times – 15 (16, 17) stitches.

Row 8 *P2tog; rep from * 6 (7, 6) times, end p 1 (0, 0), p3tog 0 (0, 1) time – 8 stitches.

Cut yarn, leaving a long tail for sewing seam. With large-eyed blunt needle, thread tail through remaining stitches on needle. Pull tightly and secure. Sew back seam.

EYE – Make 2

With B, cast on 21 stitches loosely. Knit 3 rows. Pass all stitches, 1 at a time, over first st. Cut yarn, leaving a long tail. Thread tail through remaining st; pull to tighten.

EAR – Make 4

Work as for Eye. Sew 2 Ear pieces tog for each Ear.

NOSE

With A, cast on 15 stitches. Working St st for 8 rows.

Next Row (RS) *K2tog; rep from * to last st, k 1 – 8 stitches.

Cut yarn, leaving a long tail. Thread tail through remaining stitches; pull tightly and secure. Sew Nose seam.

TIP OF NOSE

With B, cast on 5 stitches. Knit 2 rows. Purl 1 row.

Next Row K2tog, k 1, k2tog – 3 stitches.

Next Row Purl.

Next Row K3tog – 1 st.

Cut yarn, leaving a long tail. Thread tail through remaining st; pull to tighten. With points tog, sew Tip to Nose.

TONGUE

With C, cast on 3 stitches. Work 4 rows in St st. K3tog. Thread tail through remaining st; pull to tighten.

FINISHING

Using photo as a guide, sew knit Eyes and Ears in place. Stuff Nose and sew in place. Glue squiggle eyes to center of knit Eyes. With B, embroider mouth. Sew Tongue to mouth.

Chapter 7 – This and That

In this chapter I'll share some Afghan, sweater, accessory, and kitchen items. There are so many different types of Afghans that choosing a favorite one may be hard. The same is true with sweaters. Knit sweaters become treasured heirlooms through the years. Kitchen items include dishcloths, pot holders, and towel hangers. I recommend using cotton yarn for kitchen items since it can withstand high heat and absorbs water much better than acrylic.

Classic Sparkling Sweater

This pretty sweater is sure to become a wardrobe staple. It was knitted with Lion Brand Vanna's Sequin yarn. This would make the perfect gift or make one in several colors for yourself. Patter is written for size small with larger sizes in parenthesis. This pattern goes up to size 2X.

What You'll Need:

7 balls of 863-150 Vanna's Sequins Yarn in Sterling
Size 4 (3.5mm) and size 6 (4mm) needles
Yarn needle

GAUGE:
21 stitches plus 28 rows equal 4 inches (10 cm) in Stockinettete stitch (k on RS, p on WS).

SIZE: Small, Medium, Large, 1X, 2X
Finished Bust 37 (40, 43, 47, 51) inches. (94 (101.5, 109, 119.5, 129.5) cm)
Finished Length 23 1/2 (24, 24, 24 1/2, 25) inches. (59.5 (61, 61, 62, 63.5) cm)

STITCH EXPLANATION:
kfb (knit in front and back) Knit next stitch without removing it from left needle, then k through back of same stitch - 1 stitch increased.
ssk (slip, slip, knit) Slip next 2 stitches as if to knit, one at a time, to right needle; insert left needle into fronts of these 2 stitches and knit them tog - 1 stitch decreased.

PATTERN STITCH
K1, p1 Rib (worked over an even number of stitches)
Row 1: *K1, p1;rep from * to end of row.
Row 2: K the knit stitches and p the purl stitches.
Rep Row 2 for K1, p1 Rib.

NOTES:
1.Sweater is made in 4 pieces: Back, Front, and 2 Sleeves.
2.Left shoulder is seamed and the neckband is worked around neck edge before the rem seams are sewn.

BACK
With smaller needles, cast on 98 (106, 114, 124, 134) stitches.
Work in K1, p1 Rib until piece measures 2 1/2 in. (6.5 cm) from beg.
Change to larger needles and St stitch (k on RS, p on WS) and work until piece measures 14 (14, 14, 14, 14 1/2) in. (35.5 (35.5, 35.5, 35.5, 37) cm) from beg, end with a WS row.
Note: End with a WS row means that the last row you work should be a WS row, and the next row that you are ready to work will be a RS row.

Shape Armholes
Row 1 (RS): Bind off 6 (6, 8, 8, 9) stitches, k to end of row - 92 (100, 106, 116, 125) stitches at the end of this row.
Row 2:Bind off 6 (6, 8, 8, 9) stitches, p to end of row - 86 (94, 98, 108, 116) stitches.
Row 3 (Decrease Row): K1, k2tog, k to last 3 stitches, ssk, k1 - 84 (92, 96, 106, 114) stitches.
Row 4: Purl.
Rep last 2 rows 3 (5, 6, 8, 10) more times - 78 (82, 84, 90, 94) stitches rem.
Work until armhole measures 8 1/2 (9, 9, 9 1/2, 9 1/2) in. (21.5 (23, 23, 24, 24) cm), end with a WS row.

Shape Neck
Divide for Neck (RS): K26 (27, 27, 28, 30), join a 2nd ball of yarn and bind off next 26 (28, 30, 34, 34) stitches for neck, k to end of row - 26 (27, 27, 28, 30) stitches on each side.
Work both sides at the same time using separate balls of yarn.
Row 1 (WS):Bind off 7 (7, 7, 7, 8) stitches for shoulder, p to end of first side; on 2nd side, bind off 3 stitches, p to end.
Row 2: Bind off 7 (7, 7, 7, 8) stitches for shoulder, k to end of first side on second side, bind off 3 stitches, k to end - 16 (17, 17, 18, 19) stitches on each side.
Rows 3 and 4:Rep last 2 rows - 6 (7, 7, 8, 8) stitches on each side.

Row 5:Bind off all stitches of first side; on 2nd side, p to end of side.
Bind off all stitches of remaining side.

FRONT
Work same as Back until armhole measures 6 (6 1/2, 6 1/2, 7, 7) in. (15 (16.5, 16.5, 18, 18) cm) end with a WS row - 78 (82, 84, 90, 94) stitches rem.

Shape Neck
Divide for Neck (RS):K31 (32, 32, 33, 35), join 2nd ball of yarn and bind off next 16 (18, 20, 24, 24) stitches for neck, k to end of row - 31 (32, 32, 33, 35) stitches on each side.
Work both sides at the same time using separate balls of yarn.
Row 1 (WS):P to end of first side; on 2nd side, bind off 2 stitches, p to end.
Row 2:K to end of first side; on 2nd side, bind off 2 stitches, k to end - 29 (30, 30, 31, 33) stitches on each side.
Rows 3-8:Repeat last 2 rows 3 more times - 23 (24, 24, 25, 27) stitches on each side.
Row 9: P to end of first side; on 2nd side, p to end.
Row 10:K to last 3 stitches of first side, k2tog, k1;on 2nd side, k1, ssk, k to end - 22 (23, 23, 24, 26) stitches on each side.
Rows 11-14:Rep last 2 rows 2 more times - 20 (21, 21, 22, 24) stitches on each side.

Shape Shoulders
Work even in St stitch on both sides using separate balls of yarn until Front measures same as Back to shoulder.
Row 1 (WS): Bind off 7 (7, 7, 7, 8) stitches, p to end of first side; on 2nd side, p to end.
Row 2: Bind off 7 (7, 7, 7, 8) stitches, k to end of first side; on 2nd side, k to end - 13 (14, 14, 15, 16) stitches on each side.
Rows 3 and 4:Repeat Rows 1 and 2 - 6 (7, 7, 8, 8) stitches on each side.
Row 5: Bind off all stitches of first side; on 2nd side, p to end.
Bind off all stitches of rem side.

SLEEVES (make 2)
With smaller needles, cast on 50 (52, 54, 56, 58) stitches.
Work in K1, p1 Rib until piece measures 2 1/2 in. (6.5 cm) from beg.
Change to larger needles.
Knit 1 row, purl 1 row.
Increase Row (RS):K1, kfb, k to last 2 stitches, kfb, k1 - 52 (54, 56, 58, 60) stitches.
Work even in St stitch for 3 rows.
Rep Increase Row - 54 (56, 58, 60, 62) stitches.
Rep last 4 rows 10 (12, 14, 15, 15) more times - 74 (80, 86, 90, 92) stitches.
Work even in St stitch until piece measures 11 (11, 11 1/2, 12, 12) in. (28 (28, 29, 30.5, 30.5) cm) from beg, end with a WS row.
Shape Sleeve Cap
Row 1 (RS): Bind off 6 (6, 8, 8, 9) stitches, k to end of row - 68 (74, 78, 82, 83) stitches.
Row 2:Bind off 6 (6, 8, 8, 9) stitches, p to end of row - 62 (68, 70, 74, 74) stitches.
Knit 1 row, purl 1 row.
Decrease Row (RS):K1, k2tog, k to last 3 stitches, ssk, k1 - 60 (66, 68, 72, 72) stitches.
Work even in St stitch for 3 rows.
Rep Decrease Row - 58 (64, 66, 70, 70) stitches.
Purl 1 row.
Rep last 2 rows 11 (12, 13, 14, 14) times - 36 (40, 40, 42, 42) stitches.

Rep Decrease Row - 34 (38, 38, 40, 40) stitches.
Next Row:P1, p2tog through back loops, p to last 3 itches, p2tog, p1 - 32 (36, 36, 38, 38) stitches.
Rep last 2 rows 2 times - 24 (28, 28, 30, 30) stitches.
Rep Decrease Row - 22 (26, 26, 28, 28) stitches.
Next Row: Bind off 3 (4, 4, 4, 4) stitches, p to end of row - 19 (22, 22, 24, 24) stitches.
Next Row: Bind off 3 (4, 4, 4, 4) stitches, k to end of row - 16 (18,18, 20, 20) stitches.
Rep last 2 rows - 10 (10, 10, 12, 12) stitches rem.
Bind off rem stitches.

FINISHING
Sew left shoulder seam.
Neckband: From RS, with smaller needles, join yarn at right shoulder and pick up and k40 (42, 44, 46, 46) stitches along Back neck, 52 (54, 56, 58, 58) stitches along Front neck - 92 (96, 100, 104, 104) stitches.
Work 5 rows in K1, p1 Rib.
Bind off.
Sew right shoulder and neckband seam. Sew in Sleeves. Sew side and Sleeve seams. Weave in ends.

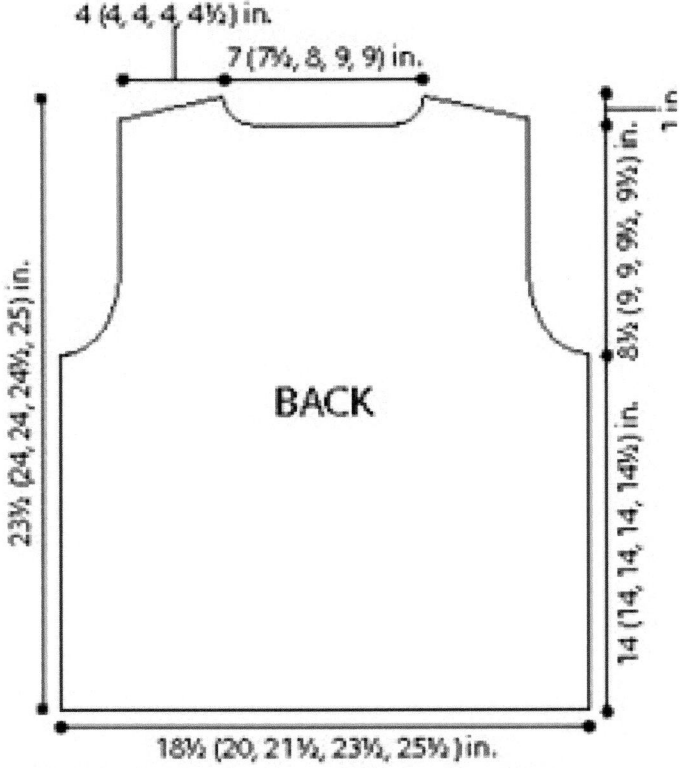

4 (4, 4, 4, 4½) in.

7 (7½, 8, 9, 9) in.

1 in.

8½ (9, 9, 9½, 9½) in.

23½ (24, 24, 24½, 25) in.

14 (14, 14, 14, 14½) in.

BACK

18½ (20, 21½, 23½, 25½) in.

ı. (21.5 (23, 23, 24, 24) cm), end with a WS row.

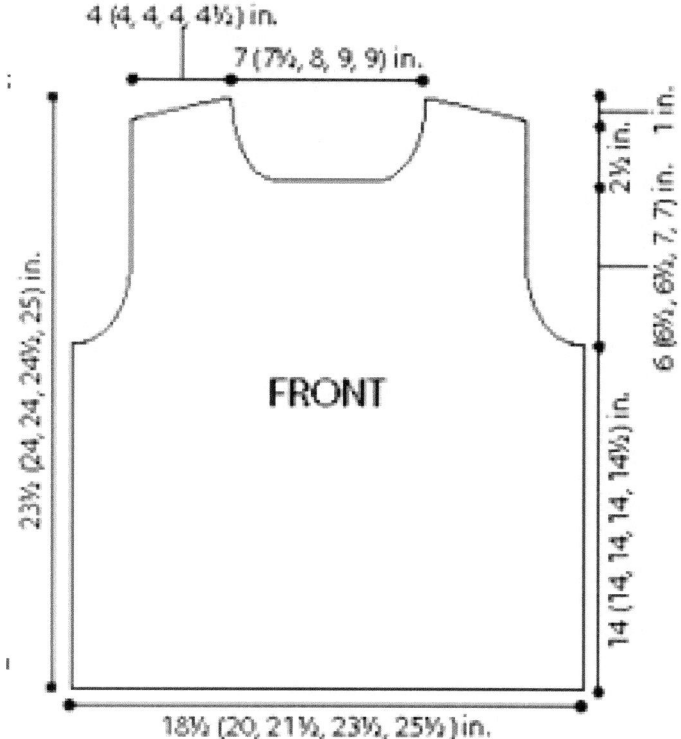

4 (4, 4, 4, 4½) in.

7 (7½, 8, 9, 9) in.

2½ in.

1 in.

6 (6¾, 6¾, 7, 7) in.

23½ (24, 24, 24¾, 25) in.

14 (14, 14, 14, 14½) in.

FRONT

18½ (20, 21½, 23½, 25½) in.

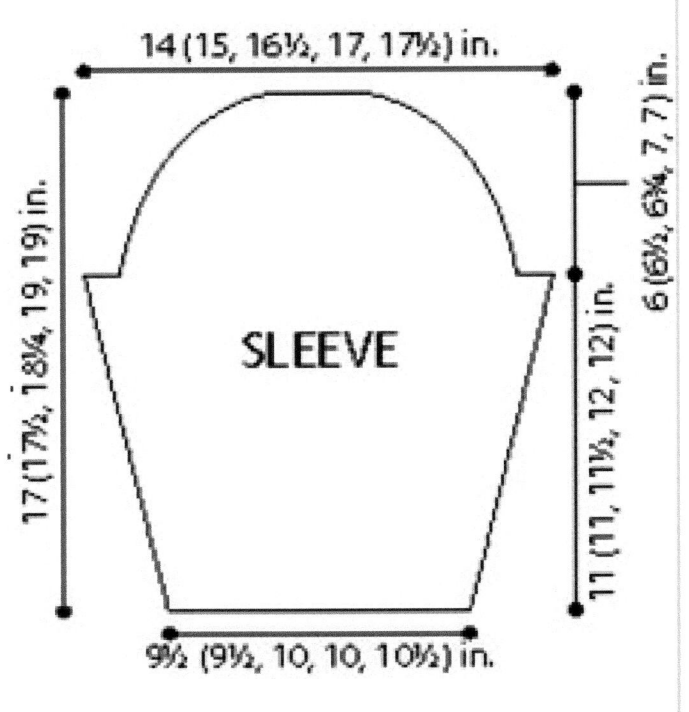

14 (15, 16½, 17, 17½) in.

6 (6½, 6¾, 7, 7) in.

17 (17½, 18¼, 19, 19) in.

11 (11, 11¼, 12, 12) in.

SLEEVE

9½ (9½, 10, 10, 10½) in.

Stripes and Checks Men's Sweater

Don't let the picture fool you, this sweater only look complicated. By alternating the colors and rows you end up with a very attractive sweater for a special man in your life. This pattern was designed by Paton's for Bernat Yarns.

Bust/chest measurement:
Small 30-32 ins (76-81 cm)
Medium 34-36 ins (86-91 cm)
Large 38-40 ins (97-102 cm)
X-Large 42-44 ins (107-112cm)

Finished bust/chest:
Small 42 ins (107 cm)
Medium 45 ins (114.5 cm)
Large 48½ ins (123 cm)
X-Large 52 ins (132 cm)

What You'll Need

2 balls for S, M, L and 3 balls for XL of (MC) (Dark Blue in picture)
2 balls of Contrast A (Red)
2 balls of Contrast B (Medium Brown)
2 balls of Contrast C (Dark Green)
2 balls of Contrast D (Medium Blue)
US size 6 (4mm) or US size 7 (4.5mm) needlesto obtain correct gauge
2 stitch holders

Gauge: 20 stitches and 26 rows equal 4 inches (10 cm) with larger needles in stockingstitch.

ABBREVIATIONS
yf equals take yarn to front of work.
yb equals take yarn to back of work.

Sl1P equal slip next stitch purlwise.

INSTRUCTIONS
The instructions are written for smallest size, larger size instructions written in parenthesis.

Note:When working with 2 colors in 1 row, carry yarn not in use loosely across Wrong Side of work. Do not twist colors around one another.

BACK
**With A and smaller needles cast on 102 (110-118-126) sts.
***1st row: (WS). Knit.
2nd and 3rd rows: With B, knit.
4th and 5th rows: With MC, knit.
6th and 7th rows: With E, knit.
8th and 9th rows: With D, knit.
10th row: With C, knit.***
11th row: With C, knit increase 4 stitches evenly across. 106 (114-122-130) stitches.

Change to larger needles and proceed in pat as follows:
1st row: (RS). With A, knit.
2nd row: Purl.
3rd row: Knit.
4th row: K2. *P2. K2. Rep from * to end of row.
5th row: P2. *K2. P2. Rep from * to end of row.
6th row: Purl.
7th row: Knit.
8th row: Purl.
9th row: With B, K2. *yb. Sl1P. K3. Rep from * to end of row.
10th row: *With B, K3. yf. Sl1P. Rep from * to last 2 sts. K2.
11th row: With MC, knit.
12th row: Purl.
13th and 14th rows: As 11th and 12th rows.
15th row: With E, K2. *With MC, K2. With E, K2. Rep from * to end of row.
16th row: With E, K2. *With MC, P2. With E, K2. Rep from * to end of row.
17th row: With MC, knit.
18th row: With MC, purl.
19th and 20th rows:As 17th and 18th rows.
21st row: With D, K2. *yb. Sl1P. K3. Rep from * to end of row.
22nd row: *With D, K3. yf. Sl1P. Rep from * to last 2 sts. K2.
23rd to 30th rows: With C, as 1st to 8th rows.
31st and 32nd rows: With A.
33rd row: With B, K2. *yb. Sl1P. K3. Rep from * to end of row.
34th row: *With B, K3. yf. Sl1P. Rep from * to last 2 sts. K2.
35th and 36th rows: With MC, knit.
37th row: With E, K4. *yb. Sl1P. K3. Rep from * to last 2 sts. K2.
38th row: With E, K5. *yf. Sl1P. K3. Rep from * to last st. K1.
39th and 40th rows: With D, knit.
41st row: With C, K2. *yb. Sl1P. K3. Rep from * to end of row.
42nd row: *With C, K3. yf. Sl1P. Rep from * to last 2 sts. K2.
43rd and 44th rows: With A, knit.

45th to 52nd rows: With B, as 1st to 8th rows
53rd row: With MC, K2. *yb. Sl1P. K3. Rep from * to end of row.
54th row: *With MC, K3. yf. Sl1P. Rep from * to last 2 sts. K2.
55th row: With E, knit.
56th row: With E, purl.
57th and 58th rows: As 55th and 56th rows.
59th row: With D, K2. *With E, K2. With D, K2. Rep from * to end of row.
60th row: With D, K2. *With E, P2. With D, K2. Rep from * to end of row.
61st row: With E, knit.
62nd row: With E, purl.
63rd and 64th rows: As 61st and 62nd rows.
65th row: With C, K2. *yb. Sl1P. K3. Rep from * to end of row.
66th row: *With C, K3. yf. Sl1P. Rep from * to last 2 sts. K2.
67th to 74th rows: With D, as 1st to 8th rows.
75th and 76th rows: With E, knit.
77th row: With D, K2. *yb. Sl1P. K3. Rep from * to end of row.
78th row: *With D, K3. yf. Sl1P. Rep from * to last 2 sts. K2.
79th and 80th rows: With C, knit.
81st row: With A, K4. *yb. Sl1P. K3. Rep from * to last 2 sts. K2.
82nd row: With A, K5. *yf. Sl1P. K3. Rep from * to last st. K1.
83rd and 84th rows: With B, knit.
85th row: With MC, K2. *yb. Sl1P. K3. Rep from * to end of row.
86th row: *With MC, K3. yf. Sl1P. Rep from * to last 2 sts. K2.
87th and 88th rows: With E, knit.
These 88 rows form pat.

Continue in pattern until work from beginning measures 16 (16½-17-17½) ins[40.5 (42-43-44.5) cm],ending with Right Side facing for next row.

Armhole shaping: Keep continuation of pattern, cast off 10 (12-14-17) stitches beginning next 2 rows. 86 (90-94-96) sts.**
Continue in pattern until armhole measures 9½ (10-10½-10½) inches [24 (25.5-26.5-26.5) cm], ending with RS
facing for next row.

Shoulder shaping: Cast off 12 (13-13-14) stitches beg next 2 rows, then 13 (13-14-14) stitches beg following 2 rows. Leave rem36 (38-40-40) stitches on a stitch holder.

FRONT
Work from ** to ** as given for Back.
Continue in pattern until armhole measures 6½ (6¾-7¼-7¼) ins[16.5 (17-18.5-18.5) cm]ending with a Wrong Side row.
Neck shaping: Next row: Pattern across 34 (36-37-38) stitches (neck edge). Turn. Leave remaining stitches on a spare needle.
Keeping continuation of pattern, decrease 1 stitch at neck edge on next 4 rows, then on following alternate rows until there are 25
(26-27-28) stitches.
Continue even in pattern until armhole measures same length as Back to beg of shoulder shaping, ending with Right Side facing for next row.

Shoulder shaping: Cast off 12 (13-13-14) stitches beg next row. Work 1 row even. Cast off remaining 13 (13-
14-14) stitches.
With Right Side of work facing slip next 18 (18-20-20) stitches from spare needle onto a stitch holder. Join yarn to rem stitches and pat to end of row. Keeping continuation of pattern, decrease 1 stitch at neck edge on next 4 rows, then on following alt rows until there are 25 (26-27-28) stitches.
Continue even in pattern until armhole measures same length as Back to beg of shoulder shaping, ending with Wrong Side facing for next row.

Shoulder shaping: Cast off 12 (13-13-14) stitches beg next row. Work 1 row even. Cast off rem 13 (13-14-14) stitches.

SLEEVES
With smaller needles cast on 44 (44-46-46) stitches.
Work from *** to *** as given for Back.
11th row: With C, knit increase 6 (10-8-12) stitches evenly across. 50 (54-54-58) stitches.
Change to larger needles and proceed in pat as given for Back for 4 rows.
Keeping continuation of pattern, as placed in last 4 rows, increase 1 stitch each end of needle on next and following 4th
rows until there are78 (86-90-90) stitches, then every following6th row until there are 94 (100-104-104) stitches, taking increase stitches into pat.
Continue even in pattern until work from beg measures 18 (18½-19-19) ins[45.5 (47-48-49.5) cm], ending
with Right Side facing for next row. Place a marker at each end of last row.
Continue even in pat for 14 (16-18-20) rows. Cast off.

FINISHING
Pin garment pieces to measurements. Cover with a damp cloth and leave to dry.
Neckband: Sew right shoulder seam. With RS of work facing, A and smaller needles, pick up and knit 19 (21-21-23) stitches down left front neck edge. Knit across 18 (18-20-20) stitches from front stitch holder. Pick up and knit 19 (21-21-23) stitches up right front neck edge. Knit across 36 (38-40-40) stitches from back stitch holder. 92 (98-102-106) stitches.
Work from *** to *** as given for Back.
With C, cast off knitways (WS).
Sew in sleeves placing rows above markers along cast off stitches at armholes to form square armholes.
Sew side and sleeve seams.

5 - 5¼ - 5½ - 5½   7 - 7½ - 8 - 8

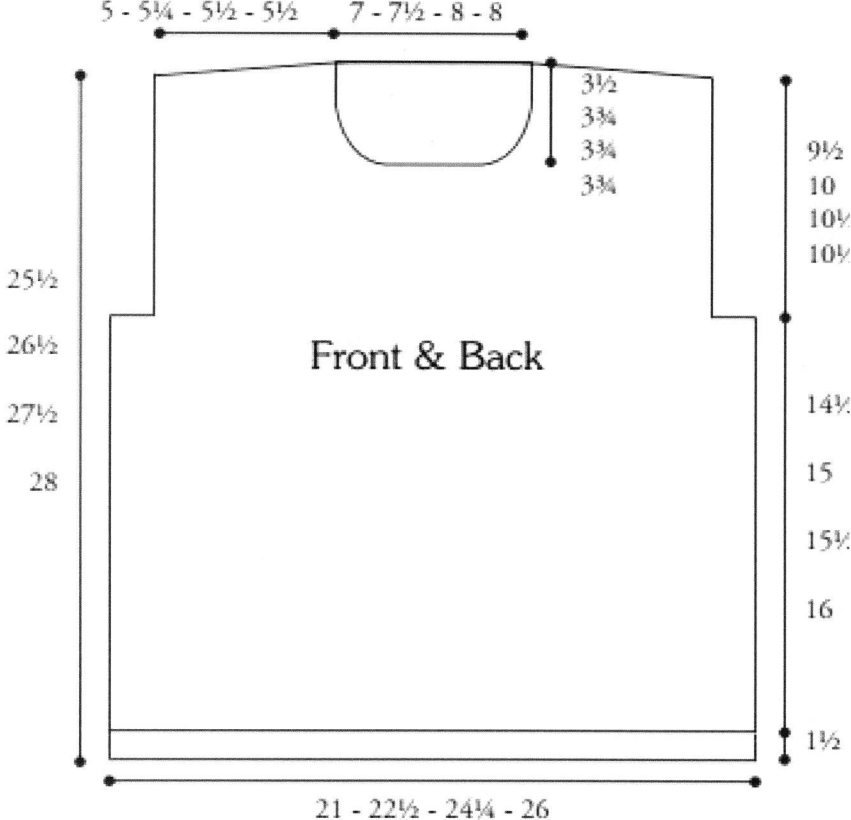

3½
3¾
3¾
3¾

9½
10
10½
10½

25½

26½

27½

28

Front & Back

14½

15

15½

16

1½

21 - 22½ - 24¼ - 26

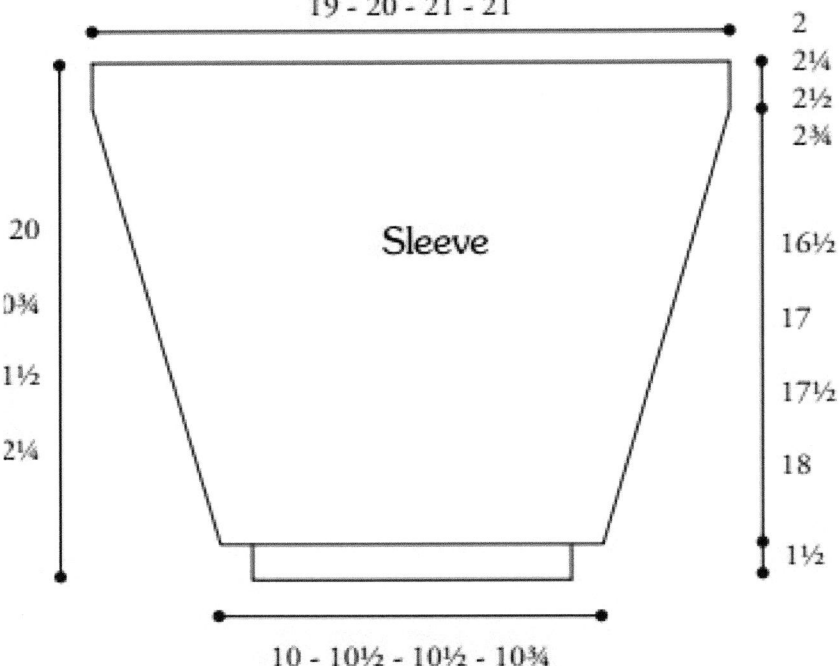

19 - 20 - 21 - 21

2
2¼
2½
2¾

20

0¾

1½

2¼

Sleeve

16½

17

17½

18

1½

10 - 10½ - 10½ - 10¾

Catch Some Waves Blanket

This pretty wave blanket is a new twist on an old classic pattern. It uses Caron One Pound yarn and will measure about 42 inches by 55 inches (106.5 x 140 cm) when completed. This would be perfect for a gift to the college freshman as a reminder of home.

What You'll Need:

You can use any medium weight worsted yarn. You'll need 16 ounces each of four colors or pattern uses Caron® One Pound (16 oz/453.6 g; 812 yds/742 m)
Grey (10505) 1 ball Main Color (MC)
Ocean (10611)1 ball Contrast A
Azure (10523) 1 ball Contrast B
Off White (10514) 1 ball Contrast C
US size 9 (5.5mm) 36 inch circular needle

GAUGE
15 stitches and 19 rows equal 4inches (10 cm) in stocking stitch.

With A, cast on 166 stitches. Do not join.
Working back and forth across needle in rows, proceed as follows:
Knit 5 rows (garter st), noting first row is Wrong Side.
1st row: (RS). With MC, K3. Kfb. K5. ssk. K2tog. K5. *(Kfb) twice. K5. ssk. K2tog. K5.
Repeat from * to last 4 stitches. Kfb. K3.
2nd row: K3. Purl to last 3 stitches. K3.
These 2 rows form Chevron Pat.

With MC, work a further 6 rows in pattern.
**With A, work 2 rows in pattern.
With B, work 4 rows in pattern.
With C, work 2 rows in pattern.
With B, work 2 rows in pattern.
With MC, work 2 rows in pattern.
With A, work 2 rows in pattern.
With MC, work 8 rows in pattern.**
Rep from ** to ** until work from beginning measures approximately 54 inches [137 cm], ending with 8 rows of MC in pattern.
With A, knit 5 rows (garter stitch).
Cast off knitwise (WS).

Holiday Teapot Cozy

You could use this cute teapot cozy all year and keep you next cup of tea nice and warm. The cute pompom adds an extra touch of whimsy. This would be a perfect gift for a tea lover in your life or if you like to share a nice hot pot of tea with a friend. The pattern is made into two pieces and then sewn together. Two sizes are given for 18 and 20 inch wide pieces to fit most teapots. You can adjust the pieces when you sew them together so the pattern is customizable to fit any type of teapot.

What You'll Need:

The pattern uses Red Heart Soft®, but you can use any medium weight worsted yarn.
1 ball of each color
Color A: 4601 Off White
Color B: 9870 Deep Sea
Color C: 4420 Guacamole
Color D: 5142 Cherry Red
US size 8 (5mm) needle
Yarn Needle

GAUGE: 16 stitches equal 4inches (10 cm) and 23 rows equal 4 inches (10 cm) in Stockinettete Stitch.

STITCH PATTERN
Row 1 (Wrong Side): Knit.
Row 2: Knit.
Row 3: K2,purl to last 2 stitches, K2.
Row 4: Knit.
Repeat rows 1-4, changing colors every 4 rows.

TEAPOT COZY

(Make 2)

Rows 1-28: With A, cast on 36 (40) stitches. Work in Stitch Pattern, working 4-row stripes of A, B, A,C, D, A and C.

Row 29: (Wrong Side): With B, Knit.

Row 30: Knit.

Row 31: K2, purl to last 2 stitches, K2.

Row 32: K2, *K2tog, K4; repeat from * to last 4 stitches, K2tog, K2-30 (34) stitches.

Rows 33-34: With A, Knit.

Row 35: K2, purl to last 2 stitches, K2.

Row 36: K2, *K2tog, K3; repeat from * to last 3 (2) stitches, K3 (2)—25 (28) stitches.

Row 37: With D, knit.

Row 38: K2, *K1, K2tog; repeat from * to last 2 stitches, K2—18 (20) stitches.

Row 39: K2, purl to last 2 stitches, K2.

Row 40: Knit.

Rows 41-42: With A, Knit.

Row 43: K2, purl to last 2 stitches, K2.

Row 44: Knit.

Rows 45-46: With C, Knit.

Row 47: K2, purl to last 2 stitches, K2.

Row 48: K2, [K2tog] to last 2 stitches, K2 —11 (12) stitches.

Row 49: K2, purl to last 2 stitches, K2.

Row 50: K3 (2), [K2tog] 3 times, K2—8 stitches.

Cut yarn leaving a 12 inches [30 cm] tail. Draw tail through all 8 stitches, pull tightly to close and knot to secure.

FINISHING
Try Cozy on teapot and pin seams together leaving openings for spout and handle. With yarn needle, sew seams together above and below spout and handle openings. With A, make a pom-pom measuring approximately 2½ inches [6 cm] in diameter. Sew to top of Cozy.
Weave in ends.

Peary Nice Dishcloth

I love to make dishcloths. The ones I knit hold up so much better than store bought, and the texture really helps scrub the dishes. These are really cute pear shaped dishcloths made with one of my favorite yarns, Lily® Sugar'n Cream. It is a 100 percent cotton yarn that is easy to work with and stand up to even the dirtiest load of dishes. Dishcloths will measure about 7½ by 8 inches (19 x 20.5 cm) when complete.

What You'll Need:

1 ball each of Lily® Sugar'n Cream® in the following colors:

Main Color (MC) Hot Green (01712) orCountry Red (01530)
Contrast ASage Green (00084) 1 ball
Contrast B Warm Brown (01130) 1 ball
4 US size 7 (4.5mm) double point needles

GAUGE

19 stitches and 30 rows equal 4 inches (10 cm) in Seed Stitch Pattern.

INSTRUCTIONS

Pear

With MC, cast on 13 stitches.

Workingin Seed Stitch Patterb, proceed as follows:

(See Chart on page 2)

1st row: (RS). K1. *P1. K1. Rep from * to end of row.

2nd row: Cast on 3 stitches. *P1. K1. Rep from * to end of row.

Last 2 rows form Seed St Pat.

Keeping continuation of seed stitch pattern, proceed as follows:

3rd to 5th rows: Cast on 3 stitches. Pattern to end of row.

6th to 13th rows: Cast on 1 stitch. Pattern to end of row. 33 stitches at end of 13th row.

14th to 32nd rows: Work even in pattern.

33rd to 40th rows: Cast off 1 stitch. Pat to end of row. 25 stitches at end of 40th row.

41st to 50th rows: Work even in pat.51st to 54th rows: Cast off 1 stitch. Pattern to end of row. 21 stitches at end of 54th row.

55th and 56th rows: Work even in pattern.

57th to 60th rows: Cast off 1 st. Pattern to end of row. 17 stitches at end of 60th row.

61st to 64th rows:Cast off 2 stitches. Pattern to end of row. 9 stitches at end of 64th row.

65th row: Work even in pattern.

Cast off (WS).

Leaf

WithA, cast on 3 stitches.

1st row: (RS). (K1. yo) twice. K1. 5 stitches.

2nd and alt rows: Purl.

3rd row: K2. yo. K1. yo. K2. 7 stitches.

5th row: K3. yo. K1. yo. K3. 9 stitches.

7th row: K4. yo. K1. yo. K4. 11 stitches.

9th row: K5. yo. K1. yo. K5. 13 stitches.

11th and 13th rows: Knit.

15th row: K5. Sl2. K1. P2sso. K5. 11 stitches.

17th row: K4. Sl2. K1. P2sso. K4. 9 stitches.

19th row: K3. Sl2. K1. P2sso. K3. 7 stitches.

21st row: K2. Sl2. K1. P2sso. K2. 5 stitches.

23rd row: K1. Sl2. K1. P2sso. K1. 3 stitches.

25th row: Sl2. K1. P2sso.

Fasten off. Sew Leaf to top of Pear.

Hanging Loop

With B, cast on 15 stitches. Cast off. Fold Loop in half and sew to top of the Pear.

Key

☐ = Knit on RS rows. Purl on WS rows.

⊟ = Purl on RS rows. Knit on WS rows.

Chart

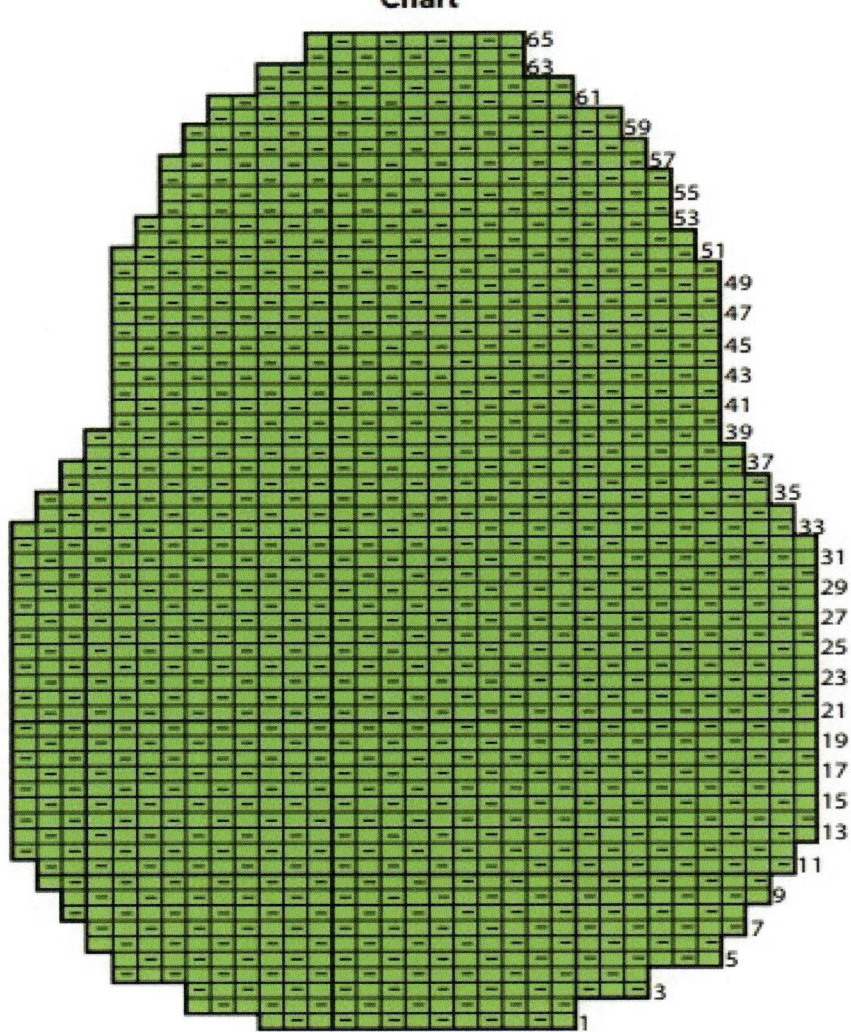

65
63
61
59
57
55
53
51
49
47
45
43
41
39
37
35
33
31
29
27
25
23
21
19
17
15
13
11
9
7
5
3
1

Start Here

Double Thick Dishcloth (or Washcloth)

These double thick squish dishcloths would also make great washcloths. Made with Lily® Sugar'n Cream® 100 percent cotton yarn they soak up water and make great suds. Since they are knitted with a row of knit and a row of purl they work up quickly. You could easily make one for every day of the week.

What You'll Need:

1 ball of your choice of Lily® Sugar'n Cream® Solids (2.5 oz/70.9 g; 120 yds/109 m) or Ombres (2 oz/56.7 g; 95 yds/86 m)
US size 7 (4.5mm) needle

GAUGE
26 stitches and 32 rows equal 4inches (10 cm) in pattern.

Dishcloths work up to be about 8 inches square when completed.

Cast on 34 stitches.
1st row: (WS) *K1. Inc 1. Rep from * to end of row. 51 stitches.
2nd row: K1. *Sl1. K1. Rep from * to end of row.
3rd row: K1. *P1. K1. Rep from * to end of row.
Rep last 2 rows for pattern.
Continue in pattern until work from beg measures 8 inches [20.5 cm] ending with a WS row.
Next row: (RS) *K1. K2tog. Rep from * to end of row. 34 stitches.
Cast off knitwise (WS).

Ruffle Pillow

This is a really feminine pillow that adds a touch of class and fun to any room. Knitted with Red Heart Soft™ and Red Heart Boutique® Sashay™ yarns, this pillow is truly a work of art. It was designed for Red Heart by Trish Warrick. If you've never worked with Sashay yarn, check out the video link at the end of this book.

What You'll Need:

You can use any medium weight worsted yarn and Sashay yarn of your choice. The pattern uses 2 balls of Red Heart Soft™9440 Light Grey Heather for Color A, and 1 ball of Red Heart Boutique™ Sashay™ 1936 Waltz for Color B.
US size 8 (5mm) needle
Yarn needle
16 by 16 inch pillow form
One 7/8 inch button
Sewing needle and thread
5mm [US 8].

GAUGE: 17 stitches equal 4inches and 23 rows equal 4inches in Stockinettete stitch with Color A.

Back of pillow is knitted fabric without the Sashay yarn.

Moss Stitch
Rows 1 and 2: * K1, P1; repeat from * across.
Rows 3 and 4: * P1, K1; repeat from * across.
Repeat Rows 1-4 for Moss Stitch pattern.

PILLOW
Back - First Section
With A, cast on 68 stitches. Work in Moss Stitch until piece measures10 inches, ending with either Row 2
or Row 4. Bind off.

Back-Second Section
Work as for First Section until piece measures8 inches.
Buttonhole Row: Work in pattern across first 32 stitches, K2tog, [yo] twice, K2tog,work in pattern across
last 32 stitches.
Work 2 more rows in pattern, working the double yarn-over as 2 stitches. Bind off.

Front
With A, cast on 68 stitches. Work 10 rows in St st, begin Knit row, end Purl row.
**Attach Ruffle
Place B across right side of work so ball end is on your left and cut end on your right. Leaving a few
inches to tack to wrong side later, * insert right needle from front to back through B and
then knitwise into first st on left needle; knit both together with A; repeat from * across. Cut B, leaving a
few inches to tack to wrong side.
Work 9 rows St st with A, begin Purl row, end Purl row.
Repeat from ** until there are 8 ruffles, then repeat ruffle only once more – 9 ruffles. Purl 1 row A. Bind
off.

Finishing
Weave in loose ends of A. Tack cut ends of B to wrong side. Sew Backs to top, bottom, and sides of Front
(but not to each other). Backs should overlap. Sew button opposite buttonhole.

End Notes

I hope you have enjoyed this book. I really enjoyed finding patterns to share with you. There are hundreds, if not thousands, of free patterns available for every project at every skill level. All of the patterns in this book are freely available and to my knowledge not under any copyright restrictions. I have made every effort to retain the complete instructions and information on each pattern included in this book.

My goal is to help you discover the fun and creativity knitting offers. The review at the beginning of this book is to help you refresh your skills. If you need more in depth instruction be sure to check out my three volume box set, The Complete Guide on How to Knit. From Beginner to Expert. Knitting for Everyone. Including Tons of Detailed Pictures: Knitting from A to Z. Take Your Skills from Basic to Advance, which takes you from complete beginner to expert level.

Thank you again for purchasing this book.

All my best,

Kathy Wilston

Amazing Patterns Attributions

Images

Front Page Image
https://www.flickr.com/photos/pandatomic/6291166233
Image from Flickr shared by pandatomic under Creative Commons License
https://creativecommons.org/licenses/by-sa/2.0/

Knitting Needle Sizes
http://www.craftyarncouncil.com/hooks.html
Image from Craft Yarn Council

Yarn Weights
http://www.craftyarncouncil.com/label.html
Image from Craft Yarn Council

Yarn Label Example
http://www.craftyarncouncil.com/label.html
Image from Craft Yarn Council

Yarn Stash
http://www.pinterest.com/pin/210402613816556230/
Image from Pinterest shared by Fresh Stitches

Long Tail Cast On
http://www.knitty.com/ISSUEsummer05/FEATsum05TT.html
Image from Knitty.com tutorial

Casting or Binding Off 2 & 3
http://www.lionbrand.com/faq/74.html
Images from Lion Brand Yarns

Knit Stitch
http://www.lionbrand.com/cgi-bin/faq-search.cgi?store equal/stores/eyarn&learnToKnit equal1&V2 equal1
Images from Lion Brand Yarns

Purl Stitch
http://www.lionbrand.com/faq/85.html?www equal1&lbc equal&language equal
Images from Lion Brand Yarns

Knitting Pattern Abbreviations
http://www.jjsknittingknook.com/faq/index.php?p equaldefault&cat equal2
Image from JJS Knitting Knook

Pattern Example
http://tutorials.knitpicks.com/wptutorials/pattern-reading/
Image from Knit Picks Tutorial

Images for Patterns were taken from pattern link.

Videos

Magic Loop Knitting Tutorial
http://www.allfreeknitting.com/video-basics/magic-loop-knitting-method
All Free Knittng

How to Cast-On: Long Tail Cast On
https://www.youtube.com/watch?v equalTw3lqx1UaDY#t equal19
KnittingHelp.com

Knitting 101: How to Bind Off for Beginners
https://www.youtube.com/watch?v equaleAMEJD2Q4hY
New Stitch a Day

How to Bind Off
https://www.youtube.com/watch?feature equalplayer_embedded&v equalAuE6Wjzq2d8
Lion Brand Yarns

How to Create a Knit Stitch
https://www.youtube.com/watch?v equalgvd8VfvNW9Q
Lion Brand Yarns

How to Create a Purl Stitch
https://www.youtube.com/watch?feature equalplayer_embedded&v equalqLVPe4zdfqs
Lion Brand Yarns

Learn How to Knit with SashayYarn
https://www.youtube.com/watch?v equallVA4OjNAIjc&feature equalyoutu.be
Red Heart

Pattern Links

Chunky Colorful Cowl
http://www.redheart.com/free-patterns/chunky-colorful-cowl
Red Heart

Candi's Checked Cowl
http://www.redheart.com/free-patterns/candi%E2%80%99s-checked-cowl
Red Heart

Survival Cowl
http://www.redheart.com/free-patterns/survival-cowl
Red Heart

Simple Mobius Cowl
http://www.lionbrand.com/patterns/L40374.html?noImages **equal**
Lion Brand Yarns

Mobius Tube Scarf
http://www.lionbrand.com/patterns/kls-tubeScarf.html?noImages equal
Lion Brand Yarns

Basket weave Scarf
http://www.redheart.com/free-patterns/basketweave-scarf-0
Red Heart

Advanced Beginner Scarf
http://www.lionbrand.com/patterns/L40194.html?noImages equal
Lion Brand Yarns

Reversible Cable Scarf
http://www.redheart.com/free-patterns/reversible-cable-scarf-0
Red Heart

Hooray Team Scarf
http://www.redheart.com/free-patterns/hooray-team-scarf-0
Red Heart

Dewdrop Scarf
http://www.redheart.com/free-patterns/dewdrop-scarf
Red Heart

Acorn Hat
http://www.yarnspirations.com/patterns/acorn-hat.html
Bernat Yarnspirations

Holy Roller! Hat
http://knittingwithschnapps.blogspot.com/2014/05/introducing-holey-roller.html
Knitting with Schnapps Blog

His Skull Cap
http://www.redheart.com/free-patterns/his-skull-hat
Red Heart

Seed Banded Slouch Hat
http://www.lionbrand.com/patterns/L40138.html?noImages equal
Lion Brand Yarns

Diagonal Stitch Pom Pom Hat
http://www.yarnspirations.com/patterns/diagonal-stitch-pompom-hat.html
Bernat Yarnspirations

Family Striped Beanies
http://www.yarnspirations.com/patterns/family-striped-beanies.html
Bernat Yarnspirations

Crisscross Headband
http://www.redheart.com/free-patterns/crisscross-headband
Red Heart

Garter Stitch Hat
http://www.lionbrand.com/patterns/L40189.html?noImages equal
Lion Brand Yarns

Romancing the Hat
http://www.redheart.com/free-patterns/romancing-hat
Red Heart

Bernat Baby Coordinates Knit Afghan
http://www.yarnspirations.com/patterns/afghan.html
Bernat Yarnspirations

Baby Love Diagonal Baby Afghan
http://www.lionbrand.com/patterns/60241.html
Lion Brand Yarn

Baby Swing Coat
http://www.redheart.com/free-patterns/baby-swing-coat
Red Heart

Mixed Baby Stripe Throw
http://www.lionbrand.com/patterns/L10195.html
Lion Brand Yarn

Feather and Fan Blanket
http://www.yarnspirations.com/patterns/feather-and-fan-blanket-to-knit.html
Bernat Yarnspirations

Knit Shell Bunting
http://www.lionbrand.com/patterns/kja-shellBunting.html
Lion Brand Yarn

Bunny Pillow Pal
http://www.redheart.com/free-patterns/bunny-pillow-pal
Red Heart

Baby Fair Isle Hat
http://www.redheart.com/free-patterns/knit-baby-fair-isle-hat
Red Heart

Panda Bear Hat
http://www.lionbrand.com/patterns/klsu-pandaHat.html
Lion Brand Yarns

Classic Sparkling Sweater
http://www.lionbrand.com/patterns/L20329.html
Lion Brand Yarns

Stripes and Checks Men's Sweater
http://www.yarnspirations.com/patterns/stripes-and-checks.html
Bernat Yarnspirations

Catch Some Waves Blanket
http://www.yarnspirations.com/patterns/catch-some-waves-blanket.htm
Bernat Yarnspirations

Holiday Teapot Cozy
http://www.redheart.com/free-patterns/holiday-teapot-cozy
Red Heart

Peary Nice Dishcloth
http://www.yarnspirations.com/patterns/pear-y-nice-dishcloth.html
Bernat Yarnspirations

Double Thick Dishcloth
http://www.yarnspirations.com/patterns/double-thick-dishcloth.html
Bernat Yarnspirations

Ruffle Pillow
http://www.redheart.com/free-patterns/ruffle-pillow
Red Heart

CPSIA information can be obtained at www.ICGtesting.com
Printed in the USA
LVIW01n1451090117
520311LV00007B/79

9781502899712